HOME
SWEETER
HOME

HOME
SWEETER
HOME

Creating a Haven
of Simplicity and Spirit

by

Jann Mitchell

With a Foreword by
Jack Canfield

BEYOND
WORDS
Publishing
I N C

Beyond Words Publishing, Inc.
4443 NE Airport Road
Hillsboro, Oregon 97124-6074
503-693-8700
1-800-284-9673

Much of the material in this book originally appeared in Jann Mitchell's "Relating" columns in *The Sunday Oregonian*. The author wishes to thank Editor Sandra Mims Rowe for her enthusiastic support and gracious permission to use this copyrighted material. The sources for excerpts from other works are listed in the bibliography in the back of the book.

Design: Connie Lightner
Typesetting: William H. Brunson Typography Services
Illustrations: Lydia Hess
Proofreading: Marvin Moore

Printed in Canada
Distributed to the book trade by Publishers Group West

The corporate mission of Beyond Words Publishing, Inc.:
> *Inspire to Integrity*

Library of Congress Cataloging-in-Publication Data
Mitchell, Jann
　　　Home sweeter home : creating a haven of simplicity and spirit / by Jann Mitchell ; Jack Canfield, foreword.
　　　　　　p.　cm.
　　　Includes bibliographical references.
　　　ISBN 1-885223-33-1 (pbk.)
　　　1. Home—Religious aspects.　2. Simplicity—Religious aspects.
　　3. Spiritual life.　I. Title.
　　BL588.M57　1996
　　248—dc20　　　　　　　　　　　　　　　　　96-4161
　　　　　　　　　　　　　　　　　　　　　　　　　CIP

For my mother,
Janice Marlin Dailey Mitchell,
who made a home not only
of love and laughter but of beauty
created from simple things
and her own unsung talent.

I miss you, Mom.

TABLE OF CONTENTS

FOREWORD   VIII

INTRODUCTION   IX

ABCs OF A NURTURING HOME   XII

1. SWEET SIMPLICITY   1

2. BOUNTIFUL BLESSINGS   15

3. RESTFUL ROOMS   33

4. CHEERFUL CHORES   60

5. HEAVENLY HOURS   67

6. SACRED SOLITUDE   76

7. TUNING IN TOGETHERNESS   93

8. HONORING OUR ANCESTORS   116

9. THE HAND OF HOSPITALITY   127

10. CONSCIOUS KIDS   141

11. ANGELIC ALTARS   155

12. NATURE'S NURTURANCE   159

13. CREATIVE CONSCIOUSNESS   179

14. WONDERFUL WEEKENDS   204

15. SOUL SUSTENANCE   210

RESOURCES   233

SOURCES AND BIBLIOGRAPHY   237

FOREWORD

Our souls hunger for deeper meaning, satisfaction, and spirituality. That's one reason my inspiring *Chicken Soup for the Soul* and sequels are proving so popular.

Americans are beginning to understand that there's more to life than moving ever faster, acquiring more "stuff," and achieving status.

As we move into a new millennium, we're returning to some of our old values: time spent with family and friends, volunteer jobs helping others, a sense of spirituality and connectedness with our world, a pace which allows us to savor life's precious moments.

Home is the one place where we can ensure that these values have priority. Not only can we create homes which nourish our souls, but we *must* create them in order to solve society's most pressing problems.

For more than seven years, Jann Mitchell has been inspiring devoted readers of her "Relating" columns in *The Sunday Oregonian* in Portland, Oregon. Her columns are both personal and universal, which is why we borrowed one for inclusion in *A Second Helping of Chicken Soup for the Soul.*

If the angels needed help arranging Heaven, they'd do well to pick up a copy of *Home Sweeter Home.* This beautifully written guide to simplification, satisfaction, and spirituality on the homefront deserves a place on your nightstand—right next to your chicken soup.

Jack Canfield
Co-author of the Chicken Soup *series*

INTRODUCTION

Home is where the heart is—and the very soul of our society.

But this is not a book urging women to quit their jobs and return home.

It *is* about recognizing the value—the essential importance—of home as a center for recharging our spiritual batteries and nurturing our souls.

In our frenetic, materialistic, work-is-all culture, home too often gets short shrift. It becomes merely a place to change clothes, gulp a meal on the run, and crash until it's time to get up and start the mad dash all over again.

Home can be more. Home *must* be more if we are to find peace in daily living, make a dent in our divorce rate, and protect our children from drugs and gangs.

This is a book for women and men—married or single, cohabitating or living alone, straight or gay, parents or empty-nesters—who want to enjoy family and friends more, slow down the pace of their lives, simplify their surroundings, clear out physical and emotional clutter, and find more meaning and satisfaction in the time they spend at home.

In *Gift from the Sea*, Anne Morrow Lindbergh writes of the sweet simplicity of time alone at the shore, wishing she could transport it home to a busy life with husband and five children:

....

"To ask how little, not how much, can I get along with. To say— is it necessary?—when I am tempted to add one more accumulation to my life, when I am pulled toward one more centrifugal activity."

These are questions more of us are asking—indeed, must ask—as our world grows more complicated.

As we end the twentieth century, having gained a modicum of material comfort, it's time to focus on quality rather than quantity—that we may rediscover the joy of living.

As Joseph Campbell reminds us: "People say that what we're all seeking is a meaning for life. I don't think that's what we're really seeking. I think that what we're seeking is an experience of being alive, so that our life experiences on the purely physical plane will have resonances within our innermost being and reality, so that we can feel the rapture of being alive."

When life is nearly done, we are aware that times of pure joy came from the simple, even mundane moments—usually with those we love.

Perhaps it is time to honor the Greek goddess Hestia, spirit of the hearth and fire—center of early family life. The Greeks worshipped Hestia as not just protector of the home but also of the city and state.

They wisely recognized the link between a stable, nurturing home and a sane, civilized society. We can do the same by reinvesting in the importance of home.

As the world moves faster and technology grows more complex, as careers topple, as families grow more geographically distant, as we feel increasingly overwhelmed, home is the one place we can count on.

Let us rededicate ourselves to what Dorothy knew as she clicked her ruby slippers together three times: "There's no place like home."

By rethinking what is truly important, by shifting priorities, by simplifying and returning to the basics of living, we can go home again.

ABCs of a Nurturing Home

A home which offers more than simply shelter to its occupants provides:

Appreciation, honoring of
    Ancestors, space for an Altar

Beauty

Comfort, Coziness, Convenience

Dreams

Enough (and not too much)

Forgiveness and Friendliness

God (or recognition of some-
    thing greater than ourselves)

Hugs and Honesty

Inspiration

Joy

Kids (or at least recognition of
    the child within us all)

Light

Music and Meditation

Nurturance and Nature

Openness of heart and mind

Pets and Plants

Quiet and Quilts

Reverence for the sacred in
    everyday life

Solitude and Serenity

Touch and Texture

Unclutteredness

View and Vision

Whimsey

Xtra helpings of love when you
    and others most need them

You, present to the moment, and
    those you love

Zest for living

I. Sweet Simplicity

> *What do I really need? And out went more and more things. Simpler and simpler. Stripped down, pared down, the house became alive.*
>
> —Sue Bender, *Plain and Simple*

Success and consumerism are out. Simplicity, a slower pace of life, and a sense of spirituality are in.

Those two sentences sound like the latest media hype. But a person doesn't have to pick up the newspaper to know that he or she is feeling exhausted and overwhelmed—and wondering if the increasing hassle of life is worth the trouble.

Weary of the buy-till-you-die, more-means-happiness myth, we're questioning some traditional American values. And we're learning the questions we need to ask ourselves:

- What truly matters to me?
- How is my life too complex and cluttered?
- What do I want in my home life that I don't now have?
- How can I live more simply and meaningfully?

The way to simplicity can feel complex and even overwhelming. Let's break it down. Make it—uh, well—simpler.

ENOUGH IS ENOUGH

When is enough enough?

In a society with T-shirts proclaiming "The one who dies with the most toys wins," it can seem that we never reach the saturation point. We get caught up in the eternal quest for more.

The dictionary defines *enough*: "To attain, achieve as much or as many as necessary, desirable or tolerable; sufficient. The amount or number needed, desired or allowed; sufficient. As much or as often as necessary; to the required degree or amount; sufficiently. Fully. Just adequately."

It's up to each of us to decide what's necessary, desirable, and sufficient.

We also may ask ourselves: But by whose standards am I judging these? An advertiser's? My mother's? My co-worker's? Unless we decide for ourselves, we may be caught in an endless game.

Only we can decide when enough is enough in work, love, and life. Here are some areas to examine.

KNOWING ENOUGH

Many of us devote countless hours and dollars trying to "get it." We tour India, go broke buying self-help books, flock to the latest guru's lectures, and switch therapists because we're stuck. Fine. But when do we stop searching and learning—and start putting what we know into practice? Once we've gained awareness, we needn't put life on hold until we learn more. Perhaps it's enough to listen to that inner voice and try to do the right thing.

LOVING ENOUGH

How long do we continue the merry dance of blaming each other and switching partners in search of the perfect mate? When do we understand that the euphoria of being in love doesn't last, but a more solid, mature form of loving can—if we don't bolt too soon. We can keep finding someone new and run when the going gets rough, or we can select wisely and hold our ground, knowing that no relationship runs smoothly all the time.

HAVING ENOUGH

Our consumer culture tells us that *more* means happiness. So we spend, spend, spend for fancier cars, designer clothes, larger homes, and more stuff to pack into them. But are we truly happy? Does more stuff really fill the empty place inside? Perhaps the proliferation of rental storage units suggests we have too much.

Could there be a correlation between our rampant consumerism and our spiritual bankruptcy, breakdown of the family, and increasing violence? It may be time to ponder the old saying "Less is more."

WORKING ENOUGH

How easy it is to spend hours at work, trying not to leave until our workaholic boss does! But at what expense? Family, friends, our basic sense of self. Then where are we when the company tells us we're no longer needed, thank you? Or when we retire and discover there's no one left with whom to enjoy the time? Let's remember that the office politics and the latest management technique or business buzzword aren't as important as we think at the time. This, too, shall pass. We can live to work—or work to live.

Doing Enough

When we hold ourselves to an impossible standard, we never have the time or energy to do enough. Perhaps it's time to slow down, say no, and do less of what we don't enjoy—and more of what we do. Many of us feel that our self-worth depends on continual accomplishment; perhaps we need to realize that value depends on what we are inside, not on what we do. Continual doing can prevent us from facing our feelings. Do we want to be a human doing or a human being?

Balancing Enough

Balance is a word we hear more and more as we work to reduce stress and increase personal satisfaction. But people are not pie charts. Each day, week, or even year of our lives will not necessarily break into even divisions of happy relationships, fulfilling work, and satisfying leisure. Let's look at the big picture and work for balance over an entire lifetime: happy time at home with small children; the years zooming up the career ladder; time with one's lover reaching passionate heights; time with this person knowing contentment and companionship. For all things there is a season.

"'Enoughness' doesn't mean voluntary poverty—it means discovering who you really are," points out Vicki Robin, co-author of *Your Money or Your Life*.

She notes that people content with enough have four traits in common:

- They have a sense of purpose.
- They can account for their money.
- They have an internal yardstick for fulfillment.
- They have a sense of reponsibility for the world.

Perhaps it's time to put our foot down and say: Enough is enough!

THE VOLUNTARY-SIMPLICITY MOVEMENT

Increasingly, people are defining what's enough and building their lives around it.

It's called the "voluntary-simplicity movement," and it involves not so much dropping out but opting out—out of the rat race, the freneticism, the materialism of our harried, consumptive age.

While some 4 percent of the nation's 77 million baby boomers are already simplifying their lives, 15 percent will have joined the trend by 2000, predicts the Trends Research Institute. Voluntary simplicity is a top trend of the '90s as people choose to concentrate on the quality—not the quantity—of their lives.

For some, this may mean working fewer hours, settling for less pay—and less responsibility. It may mean getting by on one salary instead of two, or living in smaller quarters which cost less and are more easily maintained. For others, it's getting out of debt. Watching less television. Volunteering. Creating one's own entertainment. Growing much of one's own food. Connecting with the community.

For these people, simplicity equals satisfaction. They've learned what doesn't create happiness; now they're rediscovering what does.

ESCAPING THE CONSUMER TRAP

You know the scene.

You send MasterCard $1,000 so you'll be below the limit so you can go on vacation and rack up the $1,000 again.

Into your suitcase you throw four skirts (and wear just three), then buy four more on your trip—plus six shirts because they were really great, even though they look a lot like all the blouses you already have in your closet.

You come home happy and relaxed—but also overburdened and broke.

Just where does it all end?

It doesn't, unless we make a conscious decision to stop spending. To stop confusing things with happiness. To stop kidding ourselves that we can fill an internal void with external stuff. To stop believing that more is better.

Vicki Robin stopped nearly three decades ago.

The child of a physician and a psychotherapist, she grew up with maids and a there's-plenty-more-where-that-came-from comfortability. She was an overachiever bound for a theatrical directorship.

At twenty-four, she met Joe Dominguez, a bright young man raised on welfare in Spanish Harlem. He had been rechanneled into good schools and realized that rich kids weren't any happier than the poor ones he'd grown up with. He spent ten years on Wall Street studying money; together, they researched the emotional aspects of it.

They wrote *Your Money or Your Life: Transforming Your Relationship with Money and Achieving Financial Independence.* The book invites us to examine whether the money side of the equation has crowded out the living side.

"We call it 'making a living,' but we're no more alive at the end of the day," says Robin, forty-seven. "In fact, we're more dead. So we're really 'making a dying.'

"We're sacrificing more and more of our lives for the whole process of getting and spending. And we're really not getting much in return."

Their work is about rebalancing this account so that our money serves our lives, rather than our lives serving our money.

The authors urge us to see money in a different way: not as security, power, love, or status, but as something we trade our life energy for. They outline a plan for figuring up all the hours that go into work (even dressing and commuting) and then detailing the myriad ways in which we fritter away our money.

Ask yourself these questions: Are those new clothes I bought on vacation really worth the energy I put into two workdays? Wouldn't it make more sense in the long run to use the same two days to reduce my debt?

Robin stresses the importance of using an internal rather than an external yardstick for gauging *enough*. When we look at what others have in order to tell whether we have enough money, goods, or what-ever, we're being external. And we're using an internal gauge when we look inward and ask, Am I happy with what I have?

If we accept the culture's precept that more is better, we'll never have enough. As Robin says, it's a psychological trap:

....

"Consumerism is one more desperate effort—like alcoholism and overeating—to fill what are basically psychological and spiritual needs with material stuff."

So it's up to each of us to decide just when enough is enough, when to jump off the treadmill.

The authors have a nine-step program for helping us do that. Then we can use money to do what's important: spend more time with our families, pay off our debts and live more cheaply, feel more in control of our lives, take better care of our planet.

If money isn't the source of happiness, what is? They believe it's service: We get enough to live on, then we give back.

The question to ask, they say, is not, "How can I get more for me?" Instead, it's, "How can I live my life so that life itself is better for everyone?"

WAYS TO SIMPLIFY

We can simplify our lives in other ways besides working and spending less.

CLARIFY VALUES

If we don't know what's important to us and what we stand for, we have no foundation on which to establish priorities and make decisions. Stephen Covey, author of *Seven Habits of Highly Effective People*, stresses the importance of having a purpose or mission statement based on our values. For instance, I value sharing what I'm learning with people who are also looking for better ways to live. My mission statement is: "I want to help people grow by sharing what I'm learning (and have fun doing it)." Knowing this, I can accept or refuse opportunities and invitations depending on whether or not they jibe with my mission. What is important to you?

PLAN AHEAD

Children are adept at living in the now; grown-ups know we must plan for tomorrow. The smart person does both. It's easier to appreciate the moment when we don't have to worry about the future. Here are some ways we can look ahead responsibly: Fill out organ-donor cards and living wills. Install smoke detectors (and check the batteries regularly). Wear seat belts. Start a college fund for the kids or grandkids and a retirement plan for ourselves. Practice sexual abstinence and, when we know we are ready, practice safe sex. Plan our escape from an abusive relationship or unhealthy work situation. Become more self-sufficient, which could mean learning to drive, pay bills, cook, grow vegetables, enhance work skills, and scout bargains.

Say "No" More Often

How often does your mouth say "yes" when your gut is screaming "no!" We save time and energy and simplify our lives greatly with this simple word. And we can learn to say it without offering a thousand explanations and without turning it into "yes" after being cajoled. See Chapter 6, "Sacred Solitude."

Give Up Guilt

The next time you feel guilty, ask yourself whether it's warranted. Did you do something wrong which needs to be righted, or are you being manipulated by another person's needs or values? Right the wrong, decide what's your problem or someone else's, resolve old resentments. Prevent future guilt by asking yourself daily, "Am I doing the right thing?"

Coordinate Your Wardrobe

Sue Bender, author of *Plain and Simple*, has simplified getting dressed by owning only white or black coordinates. No matter what she grabs out of her closet, she's "together." With her salt-and-pepper hair, the effect is striking.

You could also build your wardrobe around neutrals and one or two favorite colors. If this suggestion seems outrageous, at least try it when packing for your next trip. You may get used to the simplicity of dressing each day! Some parents with small children find it easy to buy clothing mostly in one color. It sure makes for easy laundry sorting!

Decrease Your Choices

Choice is nice, but our consumer society provides so many that it's often overwhelming. Face it: Don't you own oodles of earrings or neckties but regularly wear the same ones? How often do you play each tape or CD in your collection—or do you punch the same few back in? I loved traveling in Europe with only a small backpack and the barest of essentials. My only choices were dirty versus clean, cool versus warm. Easy. And freeing. We can narrow our choices without narrowing our minds.

Reduce Grocery Shopping

Buying in bulk enables you to make fewer trips to the store; with planning, it can be only once a month. And when you just need milk, it's easier to duck into a small store rather than a large one.

Organize Your Household

We needn't become neat-freaks. But we make life simpler if we can find what we want when we want it—and without several other items avalanching upon our heads. The simple act of putting things away in the same place each time lends a shred of serenity to our day. And where are your car keys?

Dispose of What You Don't Use

If it's not edible, useful, or aesthetic, you probably don't need it. And if you haven't worn/used/read it in the past year, you definitely don't need it! See Chapter 3, "Restful Rooms," to learn how to clear the clutter and keep it from piling up again.

STAY IN YOUR RELATIONSHIP

So a divorce will cure your problems? Think again. We bring the same old set of woes to each new relationship—often compounded by your kids and their kids and the schedules of your ex and their ex. Arrgh! Just consider the confusion that reigns around the holidays and you've got a hint of the years to come. Staying put romantically may simplify your life in ways you can't now imagine. It's at least worth a try. (An abusive relationship is a totally different matter. If your partner is abusive, there's no way to "fix it" except to leave.)

STOP RECREATIONAL SHOPPING

Many of us turn to shopping when we're bored or frustrated; indeed, compulsive shopping is a major problem for many people. Instead of automatically heading for the mall when the mood hits, we can pause and consider other alternatives: a walk, good music, a hot bath, a game with a family member or friend, or maybe a movie. If you simply must go on a shopping spree, do so in a bargain basement or a yard sale. You'll save big bucks.

LIVE IN SMALLER QUARTERS

How much time do you spend maintaining—and paying taxes on—space that you don't need? Some people find that moving into smaller quarters saves time, money, and energy—and feels cozier. Could you trade some footage of wall-to-wall carpeting for a vegetable garden? Moving to a smaller home might give you that. Or maybe you'd prefer a little condo with no yard to maintain. Let's remember the saying about how good things come in small packages.

Downscale Celebrations and Gift-Giving

Do you get caught up in elaborate, exhausting, and unsatisfying holiday or birthday preparations? Do you give more than one gift for Christmas and birthdays and worry about spending too much? If so, there are ways to simplify without skimping on meaning. Instead of a fancy meal out, hold a potluck at home and serve cake and ice cream with a few old-fashioned games for kids. Put a cap on the number and amount spent for gifts. Better yet, see what you can make yourself, whether it's a birdfeeder from scratch or a funky old chair you found and refinished. Creating a gift for someone puts good energy into the gift and into our hearts as we think of that person while working on it.

Relinquish Control

Deciding how things must turn out and what people must do sets you up for disappointment, breeds resentment in others, and drains your energy. Try to detach from those outcomes by turning the *musts* into preferences. Remember that you can't change anyone—only yourself. Everyone has a higher power—and you're not it.

And above all, always tell the truth! It saves time, energy, and embarrassment in the long run.

Appreciating the Little Things

As we pare down the clutter, the frenzy, the possessions, we become freer to savor life's basics.

With simplicity, we receive the gifts of our senses: the play of late-afternoon light and dancing leaves against the living-room wall. The fragrance of a freshly cut lawn or just-baked bread. The texture of a cushy bathmat beneath bare feet. The twitter of the proverbial early bird. The tartness of homemade lemonade.

Our simplified lives open us spiritually.

I like the way Christina Baldwin puts it in *Life's Companion: Journal Writing As a Spiritual Quest*:

....

"Spirituality is the sacred center out of which all life comes, including Mondays and Tuesdays and rainy Saturday afternoons in all their mundane and glorious detail.... The spiritual journey is the soul's life commingling with ordinary life."

As we simplify, we come to appreciate the small blessings which can't be bought. The ordinary becomes the extraordinary.

With this attitude of gratitude, we feel more alive. Each act of appreciation becomes a small celebration of life.

With such acts, we live from the center of our soul.

Simple, really.

2. BOUNTIFUL BLESSINGS

Rituals help us to live our lives more consciously.
—Jennifer Louden, *The Woman's Comfort Book*

Daily life bestows many blessings upon us, particularly in our homes.

The secret of happiness is to recognize them, acknowledge them, appreciate them.

One way to do so is to set regular times throughout our day for blessings. We can do this by creating small rituals which evoke mindfulness and appreciation of all that we have.

Rituals slow us down. They force us to reflect on the meaning of a moment or an action.

Cultures thrive on ritual. Perhaps that is one reason ours is so spiritually bereft. We go through the rituals of birthdays and weddings still, but the emphasis is so often on gifts and lavish spending.

"When our rituals turn away from the spirit and focus only on the material," notes Barbara De Angelis in *Real Moments*, "our spirits lose the road on which they can travel homeward."

Traveling homeward—to the nurturing nest of our physical homes and the spiritual satisfaction of our souls—is what this book is about.

Let's examine some ways we can bestow and acknowledge blessings on both.

CREATING THE BLESSINGS OF HOME—NOW

Bob was divorced nearly three years ago, but his duplex walls remain bare of pictures and his stuff is stacked in the corners.

When Kasey was transferred to a small city that she didn't like, she lived out of packing boxes for eighteen months until she moved back home.

Both considered their circumstances temporary. Many of us can identify with that. We don't want to be where we are, so we refuse to settle in, feather our nest, and make a home that feels permanent.

Yet when we're going through a difficult life transition, nurturing ourselves is essential. But we sometimes deny that. It's almost as if we believe that if we do make a nice little home for ourselves, we'll prevent our circumstances from changing. Not so. But we'll sure be happier while we wait for the tide to turn.

While traveling through Mexico for two months when my daughters were young, I noticed how much easier it was to handle the strain of constant travel in a foreign land if we found our "home" promptly when we reached a new town. We'd find a modest hotel, put away our few extra clothes, wash up—and then be ready to set out to see the sights. Having a home base, even if just for a couple of nights, gave us all a sense of security.

And security is what we need when we've left a relationship, moved away from our parents' home, or arrived in a new neighborhood or city.

I discussed the need to nest with Diane DeSylvia and Carolyn White. DeSylvia is a counselor who once co-owned an interior-design business, specializing in helping people make the most of their apartments. White is a professional organizer whose firm, Settling In Specialist, has the motto, "For a feeling of home now."

Both have worked with people who feel overwhelmed and who play the old "I'll start really living when" game.

"We need to start with acceptance of where we are right now," says White. "The home space is as close as we get to what's on the inside of it. Home's an interpretive center, reflecting confusion and chaos, transition, or values and stability."

DeSylvia points out: "It's not helpful to be physically in one place and to be mentally in a fantasy somewhere else. It's important to be where you are."

She suggests asking, "What means *home* to me?" Is it a comfortable place to sit and read? Well-stocked food shelves? A pretty bed? A place to entertain? A crackling fire and music? A comfy chair in front of the TV?

Define what's most important, then create it as best you can.

White urges clients who are moving to pack a priority box for each room—things they'll need immediately or that make the room seem theirs. Each family member can contribute.

Here are some more suggestions for feeling at home quickly:

- Tell yourself that even though this may be temporary, you're going to make your dwelling as cozy as possible.
- Set out your favorite things (photos, books, plants, things you most like to cook in) where you can see them and use them. The more the surroundings reflect your taste and interests, the more you'll feel at home.
- If unpacking seems overwhelming, first tackle the daily essentials: Set up your bed and clothes, the bathroom, cooking space, and a living-room relaxation spot. Then complete the room that feels most nurturing.
- If you've left a relationship, prominently display your favorite things that your former spouse may have hated and hidden. Hang that American Indian carving she banished to the garage. Perk up your bed with the lacy pillowslips he scorned. Leave your golf clubs by the door. Set up your sewing machine permanently in the living room.
- Fill in the gaps from a divorce by gradually adding pieces that suit you—even if they are garage-sale bargains.
- Rip pages out of magazines to get ideas about how you'd like your place to look. What attracts you will tell you something about your preferences.
- Add something you need to nurture—a plant, fish, or pet.

As DeSylvia puts it, feathering your nest "is a statement of loving yourself. It says, 'What I need counts,' and 'Who I am is acceptable.'"
Welcome home.

And however temporary, know that home is a blessing—one you deserve.

MAKING A HOME YOUR OWN

Rituals can help us turn four walls into special spaces. They can aid us in claiming these spaces as our own—just as they can help us through the transition of relinquishing our homes to others.

Moving in or out, separating or divorcing, remarrying or bringing in a new roommate, the departure of a child—all of these changes can be eased with transition rituals to help us acknowledge the significance of the event and find the blessings in the circumstance.

MOVING IN

Moving into a new-to-you home is always exciting and hopeful. A new home is a fresh canvas upon which experiences will be drawn, memories painted. It makes sense to mark the occasion with a ritual to state our intention and hopefulness.

This holds true whether we're moving into a college dorm, our first apartment, the house we've just bought, or a retirement center.

Primary in new-home rituals is a symbolic sweeping out with an old broom of previous tenants' energies and past misfortunes. Then a new broom is presented by a guest (or provide your own) as a symbol of new beginnings.

You may wish to break a loaf of bread as a symbol of blessing in your new home. Or to light a candle in each room, or in the living room—

one candle for each person who'll be living there. Let each speak their hopes for life in this house.

Creating a family mission statement or motto is a significant way of starting life anew; you could have it calligraphed or cross-stitched to display as a reminder, suggests Robin Heerens Lysne in *Dancing up the Moon: A Woman's Guide to Creating Traditions That Bring Sacredness to Daily Life*.

You may choose to do a Native American smudging with sage, moving from room to room, ushering out the past and rededicating your home to bright new possibilities.

Or your new-home ritual may be as simple as a blessing spoken aloud in each room, or joining hands with housemates and saying, "Let this home be a place of joy and love. Let it welcome those who enter, and let it nourish its occupants. Let this be a home dedicated to good and to growth. May it shelter not only our bodies but our souls. May peace dwell here."

Whatever you choose to do, heed Lysne's admonition to "keep it simple. If you find yourself creating a Broadway version of the Pope's visit to the United States, you may be missing the point."

Moving Out

I've always found it difficult to leave a home. (I even take pictures of hotel rooms!) All my life, I've wandered from room to room, saying good-bye to all the events, happy and sad, which transpired there.

We can ritualize that need to say farewell in several ways:

- Move among the rooms, naming what you are leaving behind in each—the good and the bad. Let the memories wash over you. Aloud, say good-bye to those memories. Shed tears if they come.
- Name what you will take with you from this home—proof that happy times are transportable in our hearts.
- Light a candle in each room or for each resident of the home. Blow them out as you depart each room. Or let each participant carry their candle through the house.
- Water may be a part of your separation ritual. Sprinkle a few drops in each room, symbolic of the tears and pain and laughter felt there. Then dump the bowl out in the yard as you leave.
- People who have lived in the home may choose to visit each room separately, but gather in the living room to share what you feel.
- You may want to ask a neighbor to take a family photo in front of the house.
- As Jennifer Louden suggests in *The Woman's Comfort Book*, you can create a "good-bye book" for whoever's moving (you, a roommate, a child). Include photos, memories, and messages from friends, neighbors, and those who've shared the home.

SEPARATION/DIVORCE

You may remain in a home after a partner or spouse has left or the children have gone off to school.

Consider such rituals as repainting, thoroughly cleaning, and rearranging furniture to make it a "new space." One man found painting to be therapeutic after his wife moved out; fresh paint marked the space as his own again, and the exercise helped him work out some anger and hurt.

You may also want to change bedrooms or to remove that extra chair from the kitchen table. Or add something new to each room—preferably something that you love but that your partner wouldn't have been crazy about. When my parents divorced late in life, my mother's attitude shifted dramatically when she sold a diamond ring to finance new furniture for her apartment. Substituting cheery and comfy floral couches for the Danish modern she and Dad shared helped her see herself and her future in a new light.

But even more important than these physical changes are the symbolic ones we make to help us through a difficult transition. Some of the above suggestions for moving in and moving out may give you ideas for your own living-alone-again ritual.

What would you like to do to redefine and reclaim your space?

DAILY BLESSINGS

Acknowledging our blessings adds joy to our lives as we celebrate our accomplishments, whether it's moving up from a C to a B on a report card, marking a birthday, or harvesting the first corn from this year's garden.

During the Renaissance, holidays in some parts of Europe provided people 150-plus days of celebration. Rulers knew the importance of breaking from one's work to play.

We can bring this holiday joy to each day as we celebrate our blessings.

STARTING THE DAY

Having a morning ritual can make the difference between having a wonderful day and acting like we "got up on the wrong side of the bed."

Here are some suggestions:

- Read a favorite inspirational piece, biblical passage, etc., while still in bed. The Prayer of St. Francis is one I like.
- Put a photo of loved ones next to the alarm clock so it's the first thing you see upon arising. (Change it periodically to keep the image fresh.)
- Reread your mission statement out loud to set your focus for the day.
- Draw an "angel card" or other inspirational word or saying from a bowl to reflect on and aspire to during the day.
- Post an affirmation daily on the mirror to inspire you while shaving or making up.
- Write your goals of the day in a journal.
- Get up early to meditate with the house to yourself—or create a moving meditation as you exercise or walk.
- Post a reminder by the door to guide you through the day, such as "Let go and let God" or "I go in peace" or "I go to meet my good."
- Take the time to bid a fond farewell to whomever you live with—even pets.

AND ENDING IT

Doorways or thresholds are historically and religiously symbolic. (Carrying a bride over the threshold is an example.)

So the front door (or the one you use coming in at night) is a good place to mark with a special sign, prayer, religious symbol, banner, or wreath—whatever has personal meaning to you.

As we enter our homes each night, we can use the doorway as a reminder to exhale the business of the work world and to inhale the comfort and love that is home. Touching the doorframe or whatever symbol we have posted there can serve as a reminder.

Once inside, we can further emphasize the transition by showering to wash away the cares of the day or by changing clothes along with our attitude. Some people enjoy taking a few minutes alone before starting dinner; others set aside a touching-base time with partner or children before preparations for the evening begin.

When tucking in our children, we can substitute something meaningful for the old ". . . and don't let the bedbugs bite." We can tell the children why we are glad they are ours. We may invite them to recount a way in which they helped another during the day. We may say a brief prayer together.

Reading something inspirational at bedtime to children, partners, or ourselves is as comforting a way to end the day as to begin it. The *Chicken Soup* books or magazines such as *Guideposts* are especially appropriate.

And as we turn off the light, we can say, "And all is well."

IN TROUBLED TIMES

Whenever I'm feeling stressed at work, despondent about the state of the world, or simply uninspired as a writer, I take a break and go on what I call a gratitude walk.

I simply walk, in city or suburb, and open myself to the beauty around me. I count small observations which make me smile or laugh or which touch my soul. I count old people walking slowly hand in hand, a bird perched atop a pole, a young father pushing a stroller, church bells pealing the hour, a woman applying lipstick not knowing she's observed, a beautifully arranged window display, and so on.

Sometimes I walk until I've counted twenty-five small blessings. But often I lose track and just enjoy—just as I lose sight of the stress, despondency, and lack of inspiration.

Just weeks before she died, my mother put all of her belongings into storage and boarded a bus for a leisurely, cross-country round-trip to visit old friends and family members. (We wondered later if somehow she knew she'd suffer a fatal heart attack at only sixty-five.)

When someone asked if the idea of such a long, solitary trip scared her, Mom answered, "No, I just surround myself and the bus in protective white light and get on."

During the precious time together when she reached my home, Mom shared another bit of wisdom: "Whenever I'm down, I just take a slow, deep breath and know that I'm breathing in the energy of the universe."

I needed all the energy the universe could provide when she died three weeks into her visit.

BLESSING OTHERS

Blessings are also psychic good deeds; we can send them anonymously. We all know the experience of being in the depths of despair, only to feel suddenly lifted. How do we know that someone didn't just send us a blessing?

Whenever an ambulance or fire engine blasts past us, we can pause a moment to send a blessing of courage and strength to those awaiting help. I'll never forget reading about a car-accident victim who was seriously hurt but who could feel the positive energy sent to him by a woman several cars back in the traffic jam caused by the accident.

I know what it's like to be an anxious family member praying for improvement of a loved one. (My youngest daughter nearly died of meningitis at five; one of my sisters has suffered two strokes in her forties.) So I never pass a hospital without sending a silent blessing of hope to those who wait inside.

Sometimes, as I marvel at the wonder of a jet high overhead, I even send a blessing to the person in seat 21F (or whatever number occurs to me at the time).

When we send such blessings, we're acting as someone's guardian angel. They'll never know who made a difference in that instant, but there's beauty in anonymous angels.

Anytime gifts are distributed (birthdays, Christmas, showers) is an appropriate time to pass along blessings. As we proffer our gift, we can state what we love about the person, elaborate on why we're grateful to have them in our lives, recall a precious time together.

This is a good way to slow down the meaningless free-for-all that is Christmas morning in many homes. Passing out gifts, opening them one at a time as others look on, and hearing the blessings adds meaning to the process and slows things down.

At children's birthday parties, consider allowing each little guest to present his or her gift to the birthday boy or girl. Invite them to say, "I'm glad you're my friend because..." or "What I like about you is..." as they offer the present. This puts the emphasis on appreciation of the person rather than on things.

The blessings that we offer are probably more valuable than the gift that is wrapped.

Keep an Attitude of Gratitude

There are two times to be thankful, says counselor/author Douglas Bloch: when things are going well and when they're not.

How's that?

The author of *Words That Heal* makes it sound simple. When things are going well, we can simply count our blessings, he says, and when they're not, we can turn lead into gold.

Many people believe that what we focus on expands. So being grateful for the good things will simply attract still more good. If we're oblivious to our present good fortune, chances are we wouldn't recognize additional good anyway.

But being thankful when things aren't so hot? That's tricky.

One spiritual law holds that in every adversity, there's a seed of an equivalent or greater good.

"The way to get that seed to grow and bear fruit is to give thanks," says Bloch.

That's not easy if we've just lost a spouse, we're out of work, our kids have us worried sick, or we're suffering health problems.

The good in the situation may not become apparent until much later; feeling grateful that it will come is an act of faith.

Think about it: Having our first spouse die or divorce us opens space for a new love. Losing an old job means getting a better one. Having a problem with a child spurs us into being better parents and working on a closer relationship. Having a heart attack or a cancer scare forces us into taking better care of ourselves.

When someone says, "I'm going through hell," the best response is to tell them, "Don't stop!" Bloch maintains.

If we see that pain, grief, and tough times are a process and that it will get better, we're less likely to get stuck in the hell.

"Keeping an attitude of gratitude in the midst of a hellish process is essential not only to coming out the other side," says Bloch, "but to eliciting good from the experience."

We have to acknowledge our pain, he points out. Glossing over it can only make things worse in the long run.

"But we need to realize that out of something horrible, something beautiful can and will emerge—a hidden blessing in the tragedy. This [pain] is not all there is to it, and giving thanks will help something greater emerge."

Here are some ways we can incorporate an attitude of gratitude into every day:

- Ask a blessing at the meal. If it's not already your custom, start it.
- Go around the table, letting each person name something for which they are grateful.

- Have each person say something they appreciate about the next person as they pass dishes around the table.
- Invite diners to remember people who are no longer present. Feel free to laugh or cry.
- Give a standing ovation to the cook—then pitch in to help clean up.
- Think of at least one thing you're grateful for before getting out of bed in the morning and before going to sleep at night.
- Show appreciation for what you have by giving some of it away— time, money, food, clothing, a special skill or talent.
- Keep a thanksgiving or gratitude journal, jotting down blessings as you become conscious of them. Bloch looks through his periodically, "just to remind myself."
- When you can't sleep, as the old song says, "Count your blessings" instead of sheep.

At any moment, our lives can be forever changed with a single telephone call, a knock at the door.

Let's look around us, right now, and be grateful.

BLESSING YOURSELF OUT OF BED

Do you do battle with the alarm clock on weekday mornings? Do you find it hard to crawl out from under the eiderdown on a dreary winter day? Would you rather be dozing in a fog than driving through it?

Welcome to Slumberers Anonymous. I'm Jann, and I can't get up in the morning.

At least not weekday mornings. I want a job where you can show up around noon—in your robe, if you feel like it.

As far as I'm concerned, the alarm clock is the enemy. Springing from the sack when it rings makes one no better than Pavlov's dogs, salivating when they hear the bell that means food is coming.

Getting up this way is not a natural act. Getting up before dawn may be OK if you're a farmer. Or if you have to catch an early plane for Bali.

The only thing worse than not wanting to get up is living with someone who leaps from bed whistling and cheery. Someone who chats with you, oblivious to the fact that you're playing ostrich with your pillow.

Scientists call it hypersomnia—the need for more than a normal amount of sleep. It's often a sign of depression, as is an inability to sleep.

My problem isn't as severe on winter weekends, when getting up early is an elective rather than a required subject—plus it gives you more time to do fun things. And it's not so bad on summer workdays, when the sun and twittering birds lure you from dreamland.

But winter—it's the pits. Dawn may break, but I'd rather be felled by a futon. I don't want to put on makeup; I want to wear mattress marks. But this attitude can make me a grouch and affect my relationships all day. So, I tackled the problem in my journal, where answers seem to appear by magic.

Barring deep depression, here are some solutions for getting up with grace Monday through Friday:

- Count your blessings before you get out of bed: your health, home, family, friends—and the job you're heading for.

- Invest in an alarm clock with a friendlier sound—or a clock radio that will awaken you with music.
- On an especially tough day, plan something to look forward to— a phone call to a friend, lunch out, a movie after work.
- Develop a routine to reduce the morning hassle. See what you can do the night before to cut the a.m. confusion. If you're responsible for getting others off, delegate more responsibility to them. If they run late without your constant reminding and overseeing, let them learn from it.
- If a routine is no longer useful and just habit, do something different. Eat after your shower, or vice versa.
- Keep a thermos by your bed and pour a hot cup of coffee, tea, or chocolate before arising.
- Start the day off on a positive note. Oodles of books on meditations and affirmations are available at your local bookstore.
- Drive or walk a different route to work, just for fun.
- Get some exercise. Stretch or do yoga or calisthenics before you hit the shower; go for a walk, jog, or swim; park your car or get off the bus farther from your workplace and walk.
- Take a soothing bath instead of a quick shower.
- Treat yourself to breakfast out, or stop at a different place for your morning coffee and roll.
- If you don't normally eat breakfast, start.
- Turn on soothing or rousing music to get you going.
- Hang a bird feeder outside your bedroom or dining-room window and take time to watch the birds while you sip coffee.

- Set the alarm for thirty or sixty minutes earlier, then turn it off and doze. If you're afraid of oversleeping, set a second alarm for the usual time.
- Call someone first thing and tell them you love them.

But please, do all this quietly. I'm trying to sleep.

Margot Adler notes in *Drawing Down the Moon*:

....

"Rituals have the power to restore the terms of our universe until we find ourselves suddenly and truly 'at home.'"

What rituals would you like to have in your life?

3. RESTFUL ROOMS

> *A house that does not have one worn, comfy chair in it
> is soulless.*
> —May Sarton, *Journal of a Solitude*

What makes a room feel restful? Beauty, comfort, meaning, and convenience.

A restful room makes us feel we belong there. It welcomes all who enter. People feel at home in it, even though they can't put their finger on why. "This is just so cozy!" they're likely to say.

Yet a soothing room isn't designed to impress people. If we wanted to do that, we could hire an interior decorator instead of reading this book.

Let's look more closely at the four elements of restful rooms.

Beauty. Tastes in furnishings differ, of course, or everyone's home would look the same. Beauty is in the eye of the beholder, but certain aesthetics are universal. So in each room we will hope to find at least one aesthetically pleasing thing: harmonizing colors, fresh flowers, an eye-catching picture, the soft glow of candlelight, the pleasing lines of a piece of furniture. Look around the room you're in right now. What pleases your eye most?

Comfort. If you've ever toured the grand palaces of Europe or even a local restored mansion, you may have remarked: "Gorgeous—but furniture like that sure doesn't look very comfortable!" Today, we don't have to suffer discomfort for style. Do you have a couch conducive to cuddling or stretching out for a Sunday afternoon nap? A comfy chair with a good light for reading? Dining-room chairs you can linger comfortably in when the conversation gets good? Is there a stool or table to prop your feet up while you watch TV, a place to set a glass down without ruining the table finish? If not—why not?

Meaning. The difference between a lovely showroom window and our homes is that our rooms contain meaning. This table was my grandmother's; this photo shows Dad in his uniform; this lamp is the first thing we bought together; this poster shows a place I yearn to visit. A restful room contains things important to us—items we'd grab if the house caught fire. What's meaningful to you as you look around now?

Convenience. Attractiveness counts for little if we can't find what we want when we need it. I like throws on each couch or chair so I can effortlessly cover myself when chilly. My most frequently used kitchen utensils stay handy in a countertop crock. I want a dining surface I can easily sponge off, a pile of pillows for reading in bed, an extra roll of toilet paper within reach. How does your home rate for convenience?

You and those you care about deserve to be surrounded by beauty, comfort, meaning, and convenience. Here's how.

Clearing the Clutter

Do you enjoy going home—or does your stomach knot at the chaos you'll encounter?

Now's the perfect time to clear out the clutter, make repairs, replace whatever's worn out or ugly. Perk up the place: Repaint a room, buy a new bedspread or slipcover, freshen a nook with a lush houseplant, tear down that rickety fence.

Or perhaps it's time to take the first step toward finding a house or condo instead of continuing to rent—or to scale down to a smaller place. Reach for the real-estate ads after you finish this chapter. What's the first step you need to take to reach this goal?

"Homework" may consist of simply getting organized. Start by finding a place to stash mail and bills; put things away as you use them; tackle a drawer a day. If you don't already recycle, start. Call it your gift to the Earth.

If you can't get into your garage or basement, if you have to rent storage space to hold all of your stuff, or if you can never find what you want when you need it, it's time to thin out. If you haven't used it or worn it in the past year, you don't need it. Give it to charity and claim a tax deduction, hold a yard sale or swap party, run an ad or post a notice on a bulletin board, or pitch it.

Here are ways to control the chaos and contain the clutter.

Sort the Clutter

To tackle any cleaning-out project, whether it's an attic or a dresser, follow these easy steps:

1. Get three boxes or big garbage bags and label them THROW AWAY, GIVE AWAY, and PUT AWAY. Into the first goes trash; the second is for charity or your sale; the third is for things you want to keep. Beware of the I-might-need-this trap. Remember the one-year rule.

2. Start with just one corner of the room, one side of the closet, or one drawer. Moving everything out of the room or dumping all the drawers only moves the mess elsewhere and can feel overwhelming. Working with the boxes or bags, you can be interrupted at any time and things are still manageable.

3. Carry the first box to the trash can; put the second in the car trunk to take to the charity drop (or call for a pickup); sort the third and put things neatly into logical places. (See the following section, "Organizing Creative Storage.")

PREVENT MORE CLUTTER

"Who needs all this stuff?" I found myself wondering.

So I gave notice to family and friends: No more stuff, please. Remember me at Christmas and birthdays with perishables I can use up: plants, fancy teas, candy, gourmet goodies, candles, soaps and bubble-bath, lotions, stationery, and so on. These gifts are all fun to buy or make, are inexpensive—and I love receiving and using them.

Could you make a similar deal with your family members?

KEEP PAPER IN ITS PLACE

Face it: Some of us are pile-makers. We stockpile newspapers, magazines, and mail that we intend to get around to clipping or answering or filing someday. The piles proliferate around our favorite chair. Should a mate move them, we squawk loudly.

Others of us are pack rats, saving all our grade-school report cards. Every piece of artwork the kids bring home. Recipes we never use. Ten years of *National Geographic*. There's little room around for anybody else's treasures.

How to keep paper from wrecking our relationship? Here are some tips on how to keep paper from burying you alive or sending your partner scurrying for less cluttered ground.

Mail. Put all mail into one accustomed place so everyone in the household can find it. Discard junk mail and all envelopes into a recycling bag; put the rest into at least one file folder marked TO DO or into several folders marked TO PAY (bills), TO ANSWER (letters, charitable solicitations, that chance at becoming a millionaire), and TO READ (catalogs, magazines). Monthly, write checks for all the bills. Jot the due date on the envelope where the stamp will go. Stack the bills in order of date due. Three days before, stamp and mail.

Newspapers and magazines. If you want to save an article, recipe, or ad, clip it immediately. Saving the entire publication to "go through someday" merely creates stacks and wastes time. Keep a pair of small scissors near your reading chair and drop the paper into a TO FILE folder next to the chair. Empty it weekly. If a magazine or paper remains unread when the newest issue arrives, stop your subscription and pick it up on the newsstand instead if you really want a particular issue.

Files. Most of the stuff so carefully filed away is never retrieved. Do you tend to clip and save craft ideas, travel stories, home-decor ideas, childrearing articles? Make a file labeled by category and file things vertically (horizontal files get lost in a stack of stuff). A filing system may be as simple as an accordion folder, a cardboard box, a drawer, or as sophisticated as a four-drawer filing cabinet. Keep file topics broad so you can find items easily.

Kids' schoolwork. Look over each child's work or art when they bring it home. Discard some, and post one or two on the fridge or bulletin board for a day or a week. Keep a flat, cardboard storage box for each child under their bed. Put all papers from the fridge or bulletin board into this. At the end of the school year, clean out the box, saving one piece of schoolwork and one piece of art to represent that grade. Label a covered box with each child's name to hold accumulated treasures: those saved papers, karate belt, lost teeth, locks of hair. The box becomes an archive of childhood.

Avoid accumulating additional paper: Say "no thanks" to people on the street handing out flyers and religious tracts. Refuse unnecessary confirmation letters or appointment cards—jot the dates down in your planner. Remove your name from junk mail lists (see Resources). Don't fill out surveys accompanying products—they're used to compile mailing lists.

Who said the computer age would put an end to paper? There's more than ever. The trick is to process it promptly and efficiently. Putting a piece of paper down "just for now" or because you don't know where to file it only creates piles.

Apply the three P's to all paper, from newspaper to mail to memos: *Pitch it* (throw it away, or better yet, recycle it); *Process it* (pay it, read it, answer it, pass it on, file it for later action); *Put it away* (file it, put it on a bulletin board, or put it in a scrapbook where it will be kept).

Let's not let pesky paper interfere with people!

ORGANIZING CREATIVE STORAGE

Efficient storage is an important way to keep rooms serene and clutter-free.

Finding what we want—when we want it—is easier when things are stored near the place where we use them and when we have put them away immediately after using them. (Train family members to do the same.) Frequently used items should be kept handy; infrequently used things can be stored away. We wouldn't keep our toothbrushes with the punch bowl we use only at Christmas or Hanukkah.

Organizers for closets, drawers, and cupboards keep small items in order. Stores carry a huge variety of such organizers; many malls boast stores which specialize in storage. Browsing through them will give you ideas—many of which you can create at home less expensively. Or you could buy a closet-organizer system from a closet-specialty company. Beautiful built-in closets range from about $300-up for a six-foot closet.

Let's look at some innovative storage.

Suitcases. Most suitcases sit in closets or under beds holding nothing but air. Put them to use storing seasonal clothing, hobby supplies, or games (which makes them easy to carry to the point of use). My mother, who didn't travel as often as I do, kept her family photo albums in her suitcase. In case of fire, she would have been able to grab her bag and escape with her most precious possessions intact.

Bookcases. Even if this is the only book you own, you need a bookcase. One by the door can handily hold family morning necessities: briefcases, lunchboxes, school and library books, homework, backpacks, keys, purses, mail. Elsewhere, bookcases can hold toys, games, photo albums, plants, sewing fabric, cleaning supplies, magazines, collections—and even books! Glassed-in lawyer's bookcases are great for displaying collections and collectibles you don't want to have to dust.

Clear containers. If you can see it, you are more likely to use/wear/eat what you've stored. Whatever the size or wherever they're needed, clear plastic boxes or stackable bowls make stored items easy to spot. This includes refrigerator leftovers and stored foods; sweaters, scarves, shoes; toys with small pieces, puzzles, doll clothes, crayons; nails, screws, craft or hobby supplies; makeup, medical supplies, soaps; cookie cutters, lids, candles, and so on.

Trunks and wicker chests. A small footlocker or antique trunk, painted prettily or covered with a tablecloth, can hold giftwrapping supplies, winter clothes, extra blankets, or photograph albums. If you get into it seldomly, the trunk can double as an end or coffee table. I use a rattan chest to hold gifts I buy ahead; my stereo sits atop the chest. An inexpensive wicker hamper is great for a toy box or for dirty laundry in the bedroom or bath.

Baskets. Natural baskets are cheap, fashionable, and can be spray-painted to match your decor. Use them to corral mail, vitamin bottles, hair supplies, makeup, jewelry, small kitchen gadgets, loose change, toys, soaps, yarn, fruit, and magazines. Plastic laundry baskets are also handy for toys, shoes, and catchalls in closets.

Accordion files. Pack rats, take note. These are inexpensive, portable ways to store all manner of things: bills, tax records, recipes, photos, greeting cards (file them by the month the occasion occurs), receipts, kids' schoolwork, cancelled checks. Just change the alphabetical or monthly headings by sticking labels over them to suit your needs. Mine came in handy when I planned a trip to Europe—a pocket for each country, Eurail info, maps, and more.

Filing cabinets. A simple two-drawer file is guaranteed to get the worst slob among us organized. Just add file folders and color-coded labels. I use green for FINANCES (with separate folders for tax deductions, bank statements, insurance, receipts), yellow for HOME (home-repair receipts, decorating ideas), and so on. Drop all receipts and mileage records into a file marked TAXES to make tax time easier each year. Most tax records needn't be kept longer than three years. Clean out the files yearly to keep insurance papers and warrantees up to date. Make sure all family members know the whereabouts of important papers. A couple of two-drawer cabinets can do double-duty as a foundation for a makeshift desk; just use a strong board or a door across the top. If you don't have an office area to hold your file cabinet, put it in a closet or toss a pretty piece of fabric over it and—voilà!—it doubles as an end or bedside table. Or it could hold a small TV or a birdcage.

Jewelry storage. Use a cup rack to hang necklaces and bracelets. Cuphooks screwed into a shelf or the rim of a dresser top also make handy hangers. Or post a pretty basket on the wall to hold bracelets. A cork bulletin board, with the trim painted to complement bedroom or bathroom decor, makes a fine jewelry keeper; just push plastic-headed tacks in for hangers. Poke post earrings into corkboard (which can be purchased in twelve-inch squares to glue on the wall). Egg cartons (with the tops cut off), ice-cube trays, and plastic containers that cookies or snacks come in make good free dividers for holding earrings and rings.

Hooks. Don't forget walls and even ceilings for extra storage space. Baskets, pots, and dried flowers are attractive hanging from kitchen ceilings. Stuffed animals are cute caged in a toy hammock in the corner of a kid's room—or use a hammock in the garage to hold lightweight sports equipment. Bathroom hooks hold more towels than bars do. Coats, sweaters, and raincoats on pegs on the back door are easier to locate than in crowded closets. Wall hooks can also hold mesh bags for laundry, toys, and recyclables. Take your pick from wood, cast or forged iron, brass, or porcelain hooks.

Hatboxes. Stash love letters, scarves, magazine clippings, photos, socks, knitting or crochet projects. Old hatboxes sell for $10 and up; pretty new ones are about the same. Stacked boxes in graduated sizes add pizzazz to any room.

MAKE IT EASY ON YOURSELF

Here's a way to make organization easier: Call a professional. The National Association of Professional Organizers has members in each state who can help you organize everything from closets to kitchens to offices. The average charge is $35 to $50 an hour. (See Resources.)

....

Consider: If you haven't found a place for it now, maybe you don't need it!

PLAY CORNERS

If you're the parent of young children, your entire house often feels like a play corner.

Let's look at ways to confine the clutter, make children welcome, and indulge the child who still thrives inside us all.

Specific play areas. It's possible to corral all those toys by creating specific play areas—a basement, half the family room, or the child's own room. Sometimes the latter can feel lonely; consider bunking two or more kids together and turning the other bedroom into a playroom. If you have a backyard, leave an unlandscaped portion for children to plant a garden, build forts, dig to China, and so on. Enterprising parents may divide the yard off with a low fence screening the play side.

A space of their own. Noncustodial parents who have their kids every other weekend or over the summer are smart to provide a space, however small, for those children. It says to them: You have a place in my heart and my home, even when you're not here. If you can't provide them with a bedroom, clear out part of the closet, use a special dresser, or store boxes under the bed. Putting up a small bulletin board gives them a place to keep special pictures and souvenirs of their time with you, and it gives you a place to display pictures of them when they're elsewhere.

Occupying young visitors. Grandchildren, nieces and nephews, and children of visiting friends will feel welcome in your home—and be less likely to get into mischief!—if you keep a special kids' box, basket, or drawer. Stock it with construction paper, crayons, stickers, safe scissors, and add a few books, blocks, or dollhouse people. This will keep the children busy while you visit with the adults, and it will let them know you care about them.

Your own toy shelf. Whether you're thirty or sixty-five, there's still a five-year-old inside. And five-year-olds need toys! There's room in any home for a toy shelf or play corner for your inner child. Stock it with toys you've saved from your childhood or found later, favorite children's books, a teddy bear or doll. Mine has a basket of my Indian dolls, my collection of kids' books about Indians, and a small Mexican table and chair set around which the three little dolls representing me and my sisters enjoy tea. A recent addition is a set of bright wooden stacking men from the '40s that I found for $2 at a yard sale! Give yourself permission to play by posting a childhood photo in your play corner.

Remember, it's never too late to have a happy childhood!

INEXPENSIVE FURNISHINGS

Who said furnishing a home has to cost a fortune?

Unless you're decorating with fine European antiques (and even if you are), there are ways to stock your home that won't break your budget or leave you sitting on orange crates.

OK, when you win the lottery, you may prefer to walk into a fine furniture store and just point, but for now, let's look at some cheaper ways of acquiring basic furniture, accent pieces, and home accessories.

These methods are more fun, too, because they involve the hunt, an investment of your time and imagination, and may include family history—if not yours, then someone else's.

Let's call these acquisitions furnishings with a soul.

Every family has treasures. They may not be expensive heirlooms brought over on an immigrant ship or hauled over the Oregon Trail—just something you recall fondly that's always been around. It might be Great-Gramma's rocker, Mom's sewing stand, a bench your uncle built, the bed in which your father was conceived, or that bookcase you carved your initials into as a kid—and got into big trouble for!

All these items have family history, a story—personal meaning. So why not keep them in the family where they'll be appreciated?

Ask for what you want! You needn't wait until someone dies. Many people would rather see you enjoy it. Tell a relative what you've always associated pleasantly with them or felt a special connection with. Let them know it's what you'd like most for graduation, a wedding, Christmas, your birthday, or a new baby gift.

If you're an older person, consider how nice it would be for someone younger to enjoy a favorite piece of furniture without having to associate it with the sadness of your passing. And it's a gift that won't cost you a thing. If there's a story with it, so much the better; write it down to include with your gift.

One of my most meaningful birthday gifts was the battered wooden footstool Dad made in 1952 as a Christmas gift to my grandparents. We kids used to turn it upsidedown and push each other around Gramma's carpet. My sister Sally had the stool for years; one day while visiting I commented that I'd love to have it. What a delight it was to unwrap it on my next birthday! And now my grandkids are scooting around on it.

Ask, and ye shall receive.

Make "Handmade" Your Motto

In this mass-produced, machine-made, chain-store society, it's easy to lose sight of the uniqueness of the handmade. An item becomes even more precious when we know its maker, adding both history and heart.

My mother, Janice, who didn't live to see my three grandchildren, crocheted an afghan I use when the kids sleep over. "Here's your Great-Gramma Janice giving you a hug!" I tell them as I tuck them in.

As I gaze around me, almost everything in my living room was handmade (many by craftspersons I've met): the couch and love seat by a small furniture maker in Central Oregon; a primitive log love seat made by a hobbyist; a painted bench by a New Mexico builder; a blanket chest carved in Mexico and hand-painted by me; a peeled-log floor lamp with a punched copper shade ($35 at a yard sale!); Pueblo Indian pottery; a crown of thorns carved by a New Mexico wood-carver; a sculpture by a local Indian artist, a rug woven in Chimayo, New Mexico; an afghan crocheted by a girlfriend's mother; a cow skull painted by my sweetheart.

Nothing expensive here, yet so much soul in just one room! The energies of more than a dozen artists and craftspersons enliven my space and make it truly special.

Yard and Estate Sales

Garage, yard, tag, or moving sales—they're called different things in various parts of the country, but they mean the same: Bargains!

Yard sales are usually held by a person (or group) who's uncluttering or moving. Estate sales often held by family members or professional dealers on behalf of older people who are either scaling down or who have died; they offer more variety—and usually the run of the house.

To find the best bargains:

Go early on the first day. Read the classified ads, mark the locations on a map, and plan your route. Carry sufficient cash (some people won't take checks), including small bills. Bring a tape measure along with measurements if you're trying to fit a particular space. Leave your name and number and ask to be called if an item you're interested in doesn't sell. Avoid sales advertising clothing (unless that's what you are looking for). Head first for sales in wealthy older neighborhoods or on farms. Don't be afraid to get dirty; I've been invited to poke through farm sheds and discovered some real finds. Look beyond the marked items. Some of my best bargains were found from a pile of stuff I pawed through that wasn't even for sale. I got an old quilt for nothing and a handwoven Bolivian blanket for twenty-five cents.

ANTIQUES AND COLLECTIBLES SHOWS AND FLEA MARKETS

These sales are popular all over the country. Vendors pay a fee for their space to a promoter. Quality varies, especially at flea markets. Prices do, too; you may find a pretty plate selling for $20 at one space, then the same plate for $8 on the next aisle. It all depends on what the vendor originally paid—or thinks she can get.

These sales may include over 1,000 vendors and cover acres; be sure to wear comfortable walking shoes and bring a large tote, backpack, or wire cart with wheels to carry your purchases. If you decide to think about an item, it may be gone by the time you make up your mind and return. Always write down the stall number and row number so you can find the vendor again.

Quality antique shows sometimes have a preview day, which costs a little more for admission and often isn't advertised (inquire with the promoter). People willing to pay a little more feel they're getting first pick of the treasures. And some diehards go back the last day, when prices are halved or heavily discounted because the vendors don't want to have to pack it all up again.

Find out about sales in your area by reading the classifieds under Antiques or Flea Markets in *Country Living* magazine or publications at your local antique dealer's.

JUNK SHOPS AND SECONDHAND STORES

These are fun to rummage through, and you'll find some good prices. Feel free to bargain. Many store owners are willing to go down, as long as they make a little profit. Remember, old dressers, bookcases, and chairs are often more sturdily built than newer pieces at a comparable price. Don't be dissuaded because the finish is damaged or drab—just refinish it.

CLASSIFIEDS AND BULLETIN BOARDS

Check newspaper classifieds under Furniture, Antiques, and the economy ads (the shorter, less expensive ones) for good deals. Bulletin boards in stores, laundries, apartment buildings, and workplaces are also good bets.

"But I don't know what I'm doing! I have no sense of style!" some wail at the idea of decorating.

Not to worry. We are not out to duplicate showrooms but to create an atmosphere of beauty, comfort, meaning, and convenience—which reflects our own style.

And we all have style. It's like personality—we all have one, and everyone's is different. Style simply reflects your personality, your preferences. There are no rights or wrongs. Here are some suggestions which might help.

LIVE WITH WHAT YOU LOVE

It takes many of us a while to learn what styles we're comfortable with, what is truly "us." Just look back at how your living room has changed over time—with age, marriage, a move to smaller or larger quarters, children, divorce, and so on.

When we're young and our tastes unformed, it's easy to adopt the decor of the day. Scan the background of old family photos and you'll see what I mean: prowling black panthers, macramed plant hangers, avocado green and harvest gold appliances, acrylic grapes, blue geese, sunflowers. There's nothing wrong with enjoying the latest home fashions (as long as we don't have to go back to those Victorian arrangements using braided hair!), but it's more fun to put together rooms which reflect our passions right now.

And what if you're not sure what those are? There are two good ways to find out:

1. Start a scrapbook or file folder of things that strike your fancy. Clip magazine ads and articles. Pick up paint chips, wallpaper samples, and fabric swatches from stores. Cut out photos from catalogs and advertisements. Snap a photo of a store window or floor display. As your scrapbook or folder thickens, a theme will emerge. That's what you like!

2. In a journal or notebook, make a heading: "My Perfect Room." Dream on paper, adding to the list as ideas occur. Don't worry about practicalities; just let it come. My first list read like this: A waterfall in one corner. A skylight. Lots of pretty pillows. Stained-glass windows. A loft bed with a ladder like Heidi's. Photo collages of my life and people I love. Candles and Christmas lights. Lots of books, categorized so I can find what I want easily. Textured walls. Glow stars on the ceiling. Color. Forties-style tablecloths.

Well, my home doesn't have all these things—the person living above me might object to a skylight!—but I have most of them, and I find myself amending the list with time.

Whatever style you opt for, remember that there are no hard and fast rules. Select what you enjoy; display what you love. The decorating police are not going to knock on your door!

CREATE A FOCAL POINT

Interesting, comfortable rooms usually have a focal point—either an architectural one, such as a picture window or fireplace, or a created one, such as a prettily made bed or a nicely displayed collection. Ask yourself, What is the best feature of this room? What would I like to highlight?

In the bedroom, the bed is the largest piece of furniture and thus a natural focal point. Honor it as a place of rest and love by adding further focus: angle it from the wall, make it higher by adding risers, create a canopy effect by draping fabric out from the wall. You may wish to add a calligraphed or cross-stitched saying above the bed, such as the quote from Corinthians about what love is, or even a framed marriage certificate.

In other rooms, decide what you want to spotlight. Save backstrain by drawing a diagram of the room on paper, cutting out bits for each furniture piece, and arranging a pleasing pattern—before you shove the furniture around.

CREATE UNITS

Rooms have a cohesive look when elements are tied together. This can be done in several ways:

- Arrange couches and chairs in conversational groupings so that people may comfortably talk without interruption from the normal line of traffic through the room. Close seating arrangements are more conducive to heartfelt sharing.
- A chair in a corner alone is a sore thumb, but with a stool, reading light, and end table or magazine stand beside it, it becomes a comfy unit.
- Don't shove all the furniture up against the wall. Let a couch face the fireplace, or put two love seats or easy chairs facing one another.
- Tie furniture groupings together with an area rug.

- Repeat patterns to tie adjacent areas together: a window valance which matches throw pillows, a chair cushion coordinating with a table throw, a bedspread with a matching dresser scarf (just cut a matching pillow case in half).
- Display collectibles together. Display an array of candlesticks on the mantel, pen your pig collection up in a hutch.
- One picture on a wall gets lonely. Add mirrors, small shelves, smaller pictures, tapestries, shadow boxes.

BE ORIGINAL

Any room is more interesting if furnishings aren't symmetrical. Don't box in a couch with matching end tables and look-alike lamps. Use a floor lamp on one side. Put a coffee table between two chairs.

Ask yourself about any item: How else can this be used? This gets fun. Suspend an old quilt from a rod on the wall. Stack benches to make a bookcase. Stand an antique trunk on end for a lamp table. Top an old lobster trap or barrel with a glass top for a coffee or end table. Hang a pretty rug on the wall. Display vintage tablecloths, Indian blankets, or colorful quilts on a ladder. Nail interesting old boxes to the wall to hold curios. Use a peg rack instead of a regular towel rack to hold towels (or jewelry or caps or dried flower bunches). Pretty sheets make coordinating, inexpensive curtains, table covers, and chair cushions.

RECYCLE WITH SOUL

The country look is especially good for transforming trash into treasures.

Who says dining-room chairs must match? Pick up old ones as you find them and tie them together with matching paint jobs or cushions. Plunk a plant into a lidless cookie jar or crock. Toss a quilt over a table top. Stack old suitcases for an end table. Use an old trellis or shutter to hang pictures or dried flowers on. Don't worry about dishes that match; let each place-setting be different. Stitch sheets or vintage tablecloths or bits of quilts into pillow covers or table mats. Let a weathered bench serve as a coffee table. Use ornamental old pieces of wood—brackets, cornices, gingerbread, railings—fastened to the wall as random decorations.

BRIGHTEN DARK CORNERS

Eliminate a cave effect by painting rooms a lighter color. Add a mirror, or several in different shapes, or mirror tiles. Try a white screen, a floor lamp, or a decorative wall light. Consider a sunny wallpaper for such alcoves. If you own your home, you may even want to add a window or skylight.

REARRANGE THINGS FREQUENTLY

Country decorating expert Mary Emmerling changes furniture and accessories often to keep rooms looking fresh. This doesn't mean rushing out to buy new things but simply moving items about. I store some paintings and decor items, then discover them anew every few months. Our eyes enjoy novelty. If you've become blind to your room, it's probably time to get moving!

CONSIDER THEME ROOMS

There's no rule that says your entire house must be all modern or all early American.

My condo was originally all Southwestern, which I love. But after a trip to the South Seas, I devised a tropical incarnation for my bedroom: shells and coral (some I dived for myself), fishnets, woven fans, tropical floral sheets and comforter cover, and so on. Then I changed to a frilly floral decor, and now I switch among the three as the mood suits me.

More recently, I transformed my dining area from Southwestern to country, with a quilt and dried flower bunches on the wall, a dried floral wreath, '40s tablecloths on a ladder and layered on the table, a wicker rocker, and a window valance fashioned from the border of a vintage tablecloth.

Many bed-and-breakfast inns decorate each guest room in a different style. Why shouldn't you? Variety is the spice of life!

HAVE FUN WITH COLOR

Hooray for paint! It's the easiest, least expensive way to transform a room.

Color sets the tone. And color is so much fun, there's no reason to live with drab or plain white walls.

What hue are you?

Choose your favorite color to make a room your own—remembering that there are no rights or wrongs. There are simply effects. You can make rooms look longer or wider, smaller or larger, or the ceiling lower or higher by the colors you choose. In general, light shades create an illusion of spaciousness, while dark tones make an area seem more compact. A room with little light will brighten up with off white or sunny yellow.

Paint chips can be deceptive when the color is applied to larger spaces, so it's smart to paint a large piece of posterboard to see how the shade looks in a room.

Ask yourself: What mood do I want to create in this room? And select a shade accordingly: red in a home office to energize you, a warm yellow in the bedroom to help bounce you out of bed, a serene green in the dining area to induce serenity.

It's fun to coordinate colors in a room, say with three walls one color and the fourth another. Or add a third color on the trims, wainscoting, or door.

If wallpapering seems daunting, consider easily-manageable, pre-glued borders. They perk up a room when run around windows or doors, around the ceiling, or at chair-rail height. You can even cut out part of the pattern (flowers, leaves, figures) to trim shutters, dresser drawers, cupboard doors, lampshades, picture frames, boxes, or tabletops.

To make painting easier and more fun—sometimes even faster!—try one of the popular faux (a fancy French word for "fake") finishes. Kits are available but unnecessary.

Over your existing color, sponge on another hue, letting the original show through in spots. Or apply a second color with a rectangular, flat edger instead of a brush or roller; then scrub it around with an ordinary scrub brush. I did both, with a orange hue over existing beige to create the warm patina of adobe for my Southwestern decor. You may even dab a third color here and there for highlights. This creates an interesting three-dimensional effect.

Since turquoise blue is thought to ward away evil spirits in the Southwest, I carried the look through by painting windowsills, door jambs, and doors themselves in watered-down turquoise, then wiping some of it away with a soft rag before it was dry, for a weathered look.

The same techniques work on furniture, too. And the beauty of it is, mistakes or streaks don't show. These techniques are easy to touch up if chipped or smudged with dirt—just dab a little color on.

Be bold! Red walls with purple contrast may be just the thing for you.

Fashion Wonderful Walls

Consider walls your artist's canvas—without being limited to paint.

We've already mentioned wallpaper, borders, stencils, photos, and quilts, but there are many other ways to create interesting walls and fill in blank spaces.

Consider old advertising signs or reproductions. I recently saw a laundry room spring to life with the addition of such advertisements for old laundry products.

Pretty plates needn't be confined to the kitchen. Hang those in matching or coordinating colors on display ledges or in wall-hangers on any wall in the house. Whether you buy collector plates or find treasures at yard sales, you may want to choose a theme: nature scenes, children, flowers, birds.

Bunches of dried flowers and wreaths create a country or seasonal look. Group several small wreaths for a nice effect. Combine them with straw hats for fun.

Make sport of a wall by hanging old or presently-used sporting gear: golf clubs; tennis rackets; baseball bats and mitts; fishing poles, nets, and creels; sports banners; trophies on a shelf.

Sound a pretty note with framed sheet music, old musical instruments, a picture of a favorite composer, a photo of a loved one who plays an instrument.

Have fun. Be imaginative. There's nothing you can't hang: a collection of hats, old game boards, cutting boards (especially those particular shapes), clocks, framed children's art, old baby or children's clothes.

THE ART OF FENG SHUI

Pronounced *fung shway*, this 3,000-year-old Chinese term involves placement and direction. It means "wind and water," and it is used to determine the correct placement of everything from skyscrapers to mirrors.

....

To ignore the law of feng shui, the Chinese believe, is to invite bad luck and to misdirect the environment's natural energy fields.

Honor this principle: Favor curved lines over straight ones. Have fresh water nearby. Use green plants in every room. Keep TVs, VCRs, and computers out of the bedroom. Create bright, welcoming doorways which invite energy and opportunity.

To learn more about this fascinating principle, read one of the several books written about it. (See Resources.)

Redecorating with the Seasons

Imagine a world that's perpetually summer or winter. How dull it would be without a change of seasons!

We can take a tip from Mother Nature and acknowledge yearly changes indoors to keep our home in tempo with the transitions beyond our windows.

In late fall and winter, home feels cozy and warm with dark upholstery, textured pillows and table coverings, throws handy on the arms of couches and chairs. A fire in the hearth makes us safe and content in our comfy burrows for the long winter.

But come spring and summer, we lift our spirits by lightening up. Just as we shake out light warm-weather wardrobes and pack away heavy winter clothes, we can do the same for our rooms.

We can strip tables of their coverings and clutter. Remove throws and dark pillows. Roll up the rug and let the hardwood shine. Take down heavy drapes and let the sun sparkle through. Vanquish dark paintings or heavy wall decor to the attic.

Late spring is the time to sift and sort. Cover dark furniture in light slipcovers or furniture throws. Tuck dark pillows into floral or pastel cases. Add summery touches: fresh flowers, seashells, new houseplants (put a lush one in the cleaned-out fireplace).

Our rooms—like the weather—needn't stay static if we give them the same seasonal attention we do our wardrobes. Winter: pile it on. Summer: strip it down.

....

The rooms of our homes, whether studio apartment or sprawling mansion, are living, breathing entities waiting to renew our energy. Like people, all they need is a little loving attention and appreciation in order to give their best back!

4. CHEERFUL CHORES

Still assigned the human tasks of cleaning, cooking and caring that keep us in touch with life's basics, we women know that the simple routines of life are sacred trusts.
—Maria Harris, *Jubilee Time*

How often the day seems like one endless "to do" list. We race from chore to chore, our minds ever on the task to be done next.

Too often, we feel resentment as we go about those tasks: No one but me picks up around here. Why is scrubbing out the toilet bowl always my job? How many sandwiches have I slapped together in a lifetime?

Household chores don't go away. They're ever-present, and they take time. If we spend that time in resentment, always feeling the press of the clock, we're tossing away hours which could be spent in peace.

Let's look at some ways to view "drudgery" differently.

PRACTICING MINDFULNESS

Adair Lara, author of *Slowing Down in a Speeded Up World*, recalls how her mother—who had seven children!—eschewed a clothes dryer because she enjoyed the quiet contemplation of hanging laundry.

With each piece of clothing pinned to the line, she thought about the child it belonged to.

"I carry the laundry to the basement and toss in the clothes, switching them in a wet clump from washer to dryer," says Lara. "I am doing what she did—drying the family clothes—but not getting as much satisfaction from it."

This reminds me of my delight in acquiring a dishwasher. "And what do you do with the time you save?" asked a wise, older friend.

She was right. The rich conversations and the quiet contemplations enjoyed elbow-deep in warm dishwater are lost to the hum of the machine.

In her delightful book, *Plain and Simple*, Sue Bender writes about how her Amish friends approach each of their tasks with the same attitude. She learned that any type of work could be meaningful. What mattered was the spirit in which it was done.

"There was no rushing to finish so they could get on to the 'important things.' To them, it was all important," she writes.

"Their intention is to make things grow and do work that is useful. I couldn't say exactly what the difference is, but I felt a difference. They work to work. Their work time isn't spent 'in order to do something else'—to have free time on weekends, go to a restaurant, or save for a vacation or retirement. They do not expect to find satisfaction in that vague 'something out there' but in the daily mastery of whatever they are doing."

Following their lead, Bender learned that keeping her attention on the task brought a different kind of freedom: "Satisfaction came from giving up wishing I was doing something else."

Despite how the organizational books urge us to work several tasks at once, we practice mindfulness by doing only one thing and nothing else. As our minds clear, our souls fill. This is true of any activity: chopping vegetables, sipping tea, washing the car.

As we work, we can reflect on the source of this food, the people who will ride in this car, the happiness of the child who will eat this sandwich.

And thus each task becomes a prayer, repeated over and over as we go about life's constant daily chores, just as prayer wheels send a petition to the heavens with each turn.

Today is a gift, which may be why we call it "the present." And comprising each day are countless precious moments—tiny presents to be savored, no matter what we are doing.

SHARING HOUSEWORK AND RESPONSIBILITIES

A Temple University study shows that among dual-career couples, 15 percent of the men do no housework at all. More than half the husbands work five hours or less per week, while the women put in twenty or more hours at home. Childless couples are more likely to support each other at home. And the more kids a couple has, the less men do and the more women do.

Another survey shows that women are more eager to see a man washing dishes than they are to see him dancing naked!

Not surprised? It shows how eager women are for household help from partners and children.

Sharing the housework has several advantages: Both partners reap the benefits of their work. The husband comes to appreciate the time and effort involved in keeping a home running smoothly, neither one feels resentful toward the other, and the work gets done more quickly—leaving more hours for spending enjoyable time together.

Getting everyone in a household to understand this is another matter.

The people who make a living cleaning other people's houses have several theories about why men and women argue about household chores:

- Men are used to being picked up after by mothers, secretaries, and wives, so they often don't see what needs to be done, understand why it should be done, or even know how to do it.
- Women see and do the chores because they've been traditionally responsible for the homefront. They've learned that if they don't do them, household tasks don't get done.
- Men and women often have different standards of tidiness; what looks fine to him can be a mess to her.

That's why communication about the problem is essential. And so is defining the difference between "helping" and "sharing." Helping is temporary, quick, superficial. Sharing is permanent, time-consuming, nitty-gritty.

Here's how to resolve the differences between the two:

- Discuss the problem. Talk about how your parents handled household chores and what your expectations are. Exchange views on how those expectations need to change to benefit your relationship.

- Together, make a list of what needs to be done and when (daily, weekly, monthly). Men understand time management in a work setting, so apply it to the housework as well. Discuss it as you would a business negotiation. Time each chore; you may be surprised to learn that spending just a half hour each evening can spare you a day's housework on those precious weekends.
- Make chore assignments, factoring in skill and preferences. A husband is less likely to balk if he doesn't mind the chore involved. For jobs no one likes, rotate them weekly so no one feels they're getting the short end of the toilet brush.
- Buy the cleaning supplies you need and organize them in one location. Many people feel overwhelmed and inadequate because they haven't the proper supplies and tools—or they're spread out all over the house. A small expenditure will make the work easier.
- If either person sees that something needs doing, do it.
- "Declutter" your home to make upkeep easier. Getting rid of what you don't use or enjoy and putting what you do keep in the appropriate place will make housekeeping easier for everyone.
- Follow the plan for a month, then reassess it and make necessary changes. Flexibility is important; there's little point to a plan no one follows. Involve the kids or whomever you live with.
- Remember that praise motivates and criticism discourages. Sometimes it's necessary to lower your standards, or you may be tempted to take all the duties back on yourself.
- Consider hiring a professional cleaner to teach you and/or your mate or children how to clean quickly and efficiently. Then wails of "But I don't know how!" won't qualify as a cop-out.

Home-cleaning services are proliferating like dirty laundry. If you and your household can't stay on top of the chores, consider paying someone to do them for you.

Ask potential cleaners these important questions before hiring them:

- Are you licensed and bonded and do you carry liability insurance? (This means that they have a business license and will cover any damage done in your home.) Ask to see their certificates.

- Do you have references I can check? Many people ask for references but don't verify them. Do it.

- How are your employees screened, hired, and trained? Make sure that the employees are screened for U.S. residency, honesty, and dependability—and that they know how to clean.

- Do you pay your employees' social security, medicare, income taxes, and workers' compensation? If not, you could become liable for paying these.

- Do you furnish cleaning supplies? What kind? See that supplies and methods are safe to environment and home.

- Do you guarantee your work? A "yes" means that they'll remedy dissatisfaction.

Worried about hurting the cleaner's feelings if you need to let them go? Don't be, experts advise. Honesty is the best policy. Tell the cleaner why; he or she deserves a fair, honest answer. Treat them as you'd want to be treated if you were being let go. If there is a problem with their work, tell them so they can correct it.

Here are some other considerations:

- The most frequently requested days are Fridays and Mondays. Wednesdays are easiest to book.

- Some cleaners don't do (or charge extra for) windows, ovens, refrigerators, pet cleanup, bird cages, laundry, bedding, and dishes. Ask.

- Most people give a house key to the cleaner. Conscientious cleaners safeguard keys by color- or number-coding them so a thief couldn't connect them with a name or address. Some customers leave the key in a hiding place; others are home to answer the door, then leave while the work is done.

- If your kids begin to do fewer chores, arguing that "the maid can do it," ask the cleaner to skip the kids' rooms, thus saving you money and teaching the children responsibility.

- If you're unhappy with the job, call the owner/manager immediately and be specific about the problem. Cleaners who guarantee their work will redo it within twenty-four hours.

- If something is broken or missing, contact the owner/manager immediately. Good cleaners will leave a note about broken items. Bonded or insured companies will compensate. Remember: Accidents happen and lost objects often turn up.

Maybe those seven dwarfs had the right idea when they whistled as they worked.

5. HEAVENLY HOURS

> *To restore balance, we must apply our own brakes to life's*
> *accelerating pace.*
> —Ralph Keyes, *Timelock*

Remember that 1966 Simon and Garfunkel tune which urged us to slow down and not move so fast?

We need it more now than we did back then.

In fact, it's a great guideline for this century's end. As the world moves ever faster, most of us feel more pressured, more overwhelmed, more frenetic—and less fulfilled.

So, instead of trying to accomplish still more in less time, why don't we take longer to do less? Sound outrageous? At first, yes. (I can hear you saying, "You don't know my life!")

But think again: Doesn't it also have some appeal? Think of how it was when you were a kid and you visited your grandparents: Wasn't that a more leisurely world? Maybe, just maybe, we can get some of that back again.

Just ask someone who's now walking on crutches from an accident or recuperating from an operation, heart attack, or stroke. Ask someone suffering a serious illness or even dying. They are forced to slow down.

They're not accomplishing as much, as fast. Yet the world continues to spin. And those people begin to see and appreciate more than they did before. This is a lesson which may just prevent those very same disabilities.

Living at a frantic pace can fool us into thinking that:

We're indispensable because we accomplish so much. Being a workaholic isn't insurance against being laid off. And it's often assurance of being unloved. When we're too busy, we may be avoiding relationships.

We're on a perpetual high. When we're always rushed, we're running on adrenalin—which can feel like a high. But adrenalin is meant for emergency spurts to get us out of dangerous situations. Sustained, it's not good for our bodies.

We're better employees/parents/spouses or just plain people the more we do. Many of us are actually suffering from low self-esteem, believing that our worth is gauged by how much we accomplish. The truth is, we are valuable human beings for who we are, not for what we do.

FEELING LESS FRENETIC

We can't do anything about the world speeding up, but we do have some control over our little corner of it. Here are some ways:

Drive slower. Some of us give ourselves fifteen minutes to get anywhere, and then we drive like a bat out of you-know-where to do it. Let's slow down and enjoy the trip.

Don't overbook ourselves. When we pack too much activity into too little time, we don't enjoy ourselves in the moment. Brunch with a friend on a Saturday can feel like just one more thing to cross off our lists if we've booked other appointments and errands that day. Especially during our time off, doesn't it make more sense to plan just one thing and truly savor it—instead of glancing at our watches continually and dashing off before we feel finished with our visit?

Avoid artificial timing. Our lives are filled with so many timed activities and deadlines, what's the point of living by the clock when we don't have to? We can stop trying to do two or more things at once, making every minute count, timing our jogging or whatever, even wearing a watch. Go ahead, spend a day without a watch and tune yourself to life's natural rhythm.

Be more flexible. Just because we plan to do something doesn't mean we have to do it if we feel too tired or overwhelmed or out of sorts. Let's give ourselves the leeway to postpone—and grant the same option to our friends. And remember: What we didn't get to today will still be there tomorrow.

Grant others our undivided attention. I think our kids often act up because they know we're not really listening. And most of us can relate to the frustration of trying to talk to a spouse who's reading the paper or watching TV! Instead of trying to do several things at once, let's put people first and give them the conscious attention they deserve.

Take time to do absolutely nothing. We don't need to be productive every moment of our lives. When we sit quietly, we can open the small gifts life presents and busy people miss: sun glinting off a frosty spiderweb, the dry scuttle of leaves across a walk. And this quiet paves the way for inspiration and creativity.

Let's start putting fewer items on our "to do" lists and giving ourselves more time to enjoy what's truly important.

And if we don't know what is important, we can ask the person we see moving v-e-r-y slowly.

BE WARY OF "TIME-SAVERS"

Ever notice how we have more conveniences and less time than anyone else in the world?

Like daylight-saving time, so-called time-savers can trick us into believing we have more time. We don't, of course. No getting around the fact that there are only twenty-four hours in a day.

In fact, some argue that time-savers not only don't save time but actually create more work—or at least more time in which to fit more work. How so?

Well, just think back to ten or fifteen years ago, when you had fewer time-savers such as ATMs, VCRs, microwaves, pagers, and cellular phones. Many of us have these goodies now—but aren't you even more pressed for time than you were a decade ago?

In *Timelock: How Life Got So Hectic and What You Can Do About It,* author Ralph Keyes points out four reasons why "conveniences" don't actually save time and effort:

- They convert a few big, time-consuming tasks into many smaller ones that can consume more time overall.
- They create new tasks altogether.
- They raise standards.

- They require added time to master, maintain, and repair (like getting your VCR to work).

Such devices may accomplish a task in less time, but they may also speed up our expectations, making us even more impatient—such as when we stand tapping our fingers while the microwave heats a cup of water for tea. When we used a tea kettle, we did something else until the whistle drew us back. We didn't expect instant hot water.

CREATING TIME-MAKERS

Instead of buying into rampant consumerism (purchasing more machines) and frenetic doerism (cramming in more activities), let's look at time-makers—ways to do less and enjoy life more.

Here are a few:

Say "no" more often. "No" is a complete sentence. If you find yourself saying "yes" when every fiber of your being is shouting "no," buy yourself time by saying, "I must check my calendar. Let me get back to you on that." Then get in touch with what you really want, which is to build up your courage to say no. Then get back to the person and say, "Sorry, I can't do that. I have another commitment" (even though that commitment is to napping). It's not necessary to explain your refusal.

Write a mission statement. Become clear about what's important to you. In a few sentences, sum up what's important to you, what you want from life, what you want to contribute to the world. (Stuck? Flash-forward to your funeral and see what you hope people will say about the kind of person you were.) This is your mission statement. When people make requests of you or when you have a decision to make, refer to your mission statement. It will make it far easier to say no immediately.

Remove the clutter. Eliminate the people, activities, and stuff that detract rather than add to your life. Stop lunching with friends who drain rather than inspire you. Quit doing the volunteer work that no longer stimulates you. Cease having family members over at Christmas if all they do is fight. Consider condo living if yardwork is a chore.

Schedule yourself onto your calendar. Ensure more time to do what you want by inking yourself into your schedule. Otherwise, time you promise yourself is invariably eroded with other commitments. Make sure some of this time is unplanned so that you can do whatever you're in the mood for at the time. You may not have any more hours in the day, but it will feel like it.

Avoid needless choices. Too many choices are confusing. They don't necessarily make life easier—but they do make you feel more anxious. Have you ever run into the grocery store to grab a box of Cheerios only to get lost in a mile-long aisle of cereals? I solved this problem by shopping at a smaller grocery store—especially when I'm after only a few things. Face it, we don't require a lobster tank when all we want is a quart of milk.

Relinquish control. It's amazing how much time and energy we expend trying to manipulate people and situations into the actions and outcomes we deem appropriate. Let the universe have its way and you'll have lots more time to devote to something more satisfying and effective. Let's keep in mind that everyone we care about has a Higher Power. And we're not it.

Substitute "want" for "should." Instead of obeying that chorus of *shoulds* in our heads, we can ask ourselves what we actually want. When *should* and *want* are at odds, we let *want* win. Whose *shoulds* are those, anyway—our parents', kids', partner's, boss's? We're not talking total irresponsibility, just getting clearer about how we spend our time.

OFF WITH THE TV

"KILL YOUR TELEVISION," urges the bumper sticker on a car in my condo complex.

It's not just the violence I hate—it's the mindlessness. The sheer waste of time.

Stumble in the door at night, fix something to eat, and plop down in front of the tube. Before you know it, the news is on and it's time for bed. Another forgettable evening gone.

Sound familiar?

If you need convincing, consider these facts:

- A recent British study reports that watching bad news on TV not only makes people concerned about what they see but increases anxiety about unrelated matters.

- A long-term Harvard study notes that high-anxiety men are more than four times as likely to suffer a fatal heart attack than those who are not anxious.

- According to a 1992 report by the American Psychological Association, kids under age seven can't distinguish commercials from programs; kids who watch lots of TV don't do as well in school; seeing lots of screen sex increases arousal in adults and adolescents; pregnancy and disease is ignored in TV sex, giving teens the wrong impression; racial, ethnic, and sexual stereotypes are reinforced; TV-watching promotes obesity in both adults and children; TV replaces the social interaction that elderly people need to be emotionally healthy.

Summertime, when TV shows are being rerun, is an especially good time to try breaking the TV habit. The next time you find yourself automatically snapping on the tube, pause and consider:

What could I do instead? Run through your options: Call a friend. Write a letter. Pay bills. Play music. Walk the dog.

Don't turn on the TV casually. Check the listings first to make sure there's something you specifically want to watch.

Pick up a book or magazine instead. How long has it been since you've gotten lost in an engrossing novel?

Establish no-TV evenings. Instead, play games with the family. Invite friends in. Work on a project or hobby with someone and enjoy the easy conversation that accompanies an activity. Go for a hike or bike ride. Starting a family tradition like this will mean far more to kids in the long run than watching a show they won't even recall.

Tell the children that tonight they get to turn on the imaginary TV. Tell stories from your childhood or their babyhood; read a children's book, without illustrations, out loud. Invite them to close their eyes. Discuss the pictures they "see." Is the house large or small? What color is the girl's dress? Is the sun shining or is it raining? Emphasize the freedom they have to imagine things however they want. Then they can tell you a story with as much detail as possible so that you can both use your mind's TV.

Plan long-term substitutes for TV. Take a class. Volunteer. Restore a car or a piece of furniture. Learn how to sew, shoot pictures, use your computer, write a poem, identify the stars.

Consider the longer daylight hours a bonus you don't want to waste. Take a walk in the woods. Explore a new neighborhood. Linger in an outdoor cafe. Work in the yard. Take a drive in the country.

Maybe we don't need to kill our televisions. Perhaps we could just unplug them.

....

We can watch life on TV. Or we can live it.

6. SACRED SOLITUDE

Women need real moments of solitude and self-reflection to balance out how much of ourselves we give away.
—Barbara De Angelis, *Real Moments*

"Why do you live alone, Gramma?" Ashley asked me at three.

I brushed her off, but thought about it and later explained, "I'm a writer, and writers have to be alone lots so they can think about the stories they are going to write."

Perhaps when she's older, I'll include the other reasons: I enjoy being alone. I'm through cleaning up after others. I like to invite family and friends in and savor the silence when they leave. And even though my sweetheart is with me much of the time, I choose not to live with him.

This wasn't always so. In my twenties, after my divorce, I recall crying myself to sleep because no one shared the bed. (Now I love sprawling out when alone!)

In my thirties, I remember walking through neighborhoods and looking longingly at the families inside—all ecstatically happy, I tortured myself.

It took many baby steps before I was able, as a single parent, to take my children to the beach for the day, then away for the weekend, then to venture to Hawaii by myself.

When my girls would go to summer camp for two weeks each summer, I invariably anticipated my freedom—only to feel at loose ends until I learned to enjoy my own company.

And yet, I remember the joy of having the house all to myself as a child. With five kids and two parents, that didn't happen often enough.

While we may enjoy solitude in childhood, many of us forget how to do so in adulthood because we seldom get it. We're so busy putting other people's needs first.

But we can't fill up other people's buckets when our own wells are dry. This year we can become our own parents, taking as good care of ourselves as we do our children, our partners, our friends, our elderly parents.

We can give ourselves permission to relax, to say no, to stop feeling guilty, to set limits on what we will and won't do. What do we wish someone would do for us in an ideal world? Let's do it for ourselves.

....

Solitude—time to ourselves—recharges our batteries. It allows us to reconnect with our souls, our dreams, our goals.

Indeed, all the spiritual masters sought solitude in the wilderness: Jesus, the Buddha, Mohammed, Moses, Zoroaster.

As Maria Harris so eloquently puts it in her book, *Jubilee Time*, solitude enables us to "catch our soul's breath."

This yearning was difficult to explain; it felt irrational.

I wanted to trade lives with my grandmother—my traditional grandmother who had raised three children, had never worked outside her home, had been married to the same man for umpteen million years, and had never glimpsed the world beyond a trip-of-a-lifetime cruise to Hawaii.

Why would a liberated woman—successfully doing the work she's always wanted to—long for such a switch? Perhaps it wasn't the events of Grandma's life I wanted, but the pace and the peace of her life. Leisurely breakfasts beckoning with the crisp pungency of bacon and freshly ground coffee. Long walks paced to fit a grandchild's tiny legs. Evenings of card games with friends and the soothing hum of conversation.

Carrye Dailey (my maternal grandmother) had no name recognition, no awards for her life's work, no album packed with photos of exotic places. But she had a sense of where she fit into her world. Her life had a gentle rhythm, a connectedness.

For the past few months, staying home to drink tea, watch the birds, ruminate, and write in my journal has seemed more important than work, family, or friends. After twenty-five years of producing and caretaking, I wanted to pull into myself. Nothing seemed as important, as nurturing, as interesting.

At a gathering of women, I asked whether others felt this way. "Yes!" they chorused. Some days it seemed an inconvenience to go to work, some added.

So perhaps this yearning, this isolation was normal.

And then a friend handed me a book that explained this phenomenon. A thin little paperback, passed from woman to woman. No book tour, no hype, just a book given to mothers and sisters and girlfriends for birthdays and Christmas and no reason at all.

Circle of Stones: A Woman's Journey to Herself is a little gem written by Judith Duerk, an East Coast therapist and tai chi instructor.

Her premise is that women's lives have become frantic, full of achievements, yet ultimately unsatisfying because we have adopted the male definition of success and moved away from a connection with ourselves and other women. This is no diatribe but a gentle, wise little book that speaks to the heart—and hits home.

Duerk writes about competition and quietude, about the inherent value of being a woman without constantly having to prove herself: "Woman herself has become alienated from her need to sink into herself. It is a tragic token of the lack of recognition of a separate and unique feminine process that, the more intelligent and educated a woman is, the more she may feel that she has been asked to alienate herself from her deeper feminine nature.

"If a woman is caught in an overextended lifestyle and achievement-oriented values, depression or illness may offer the only opportunity to allow her to be with herself. The issue is not whether women can achieve, but that preoccupation with achievement may deny a descent into her deeper nature which a woman must make to touch her true strengths."

Duerk urges women to take back our own feminine values, to stop denying our needs, to recognize and understand our fatigue.

Is this something women have always known but forgot once we moved into the production-motivated, success-oriented work world of men? Is the dissatisfaction, the anxiety, the hole-in-my-soul feeling so many of us have, no matter how much we accomplish and achieve, the result of denying ourselves the time to merely sit and observe and contemplate?

And I conclude from this loving book: Our grandmothers and mothers passed that peace on to us as our birthright as women. We've but to slow down, listen to our inner voice, and claim it.

The secret isn't in the lace-doily trappings of our grandmothers but in the time taken to be with ourselves, our thoughts, and our feelings— not constantly producing, but simply being.

Taking time for birds, tea, and me is like coming home—to ourselves.

MAKE A COMMITMENT TO YOURSELF

You dash out on your lunch hour for a haircut. On the way home after work, you pick up dry cleaning and a few groceries before getting the kids from day care. The kids are starving, and you're already exhausted.

A friend invites you to dinner and a movie. You'd love to go but that's the night you're helping your elderly dad pay his bills, and you can't make it the next night either because your mate's boss is coming for dinner, and . . . .

When is it ever time for just you?

Since twenty-four-hour days shrunk to about eighteen sometime when no one was looking, time for doing the things we want to do for ourselves seems nonexistent. We juggle work, home, family, and friends—and settle for whatever crumbs of solitude, thanks, or satisfaction come our way.

Taking care of everyone but ourselves breeds resentment, martyrdom, and illness. When we put ourselves last on our "to do" lists, self-care never happens. Then we wonder why we feel so out of balance, tired, and edgy. Whenever I become resentful of those I care most about, it's invariably because I'm doing too much for them and not enough for myself.

This no-time-for-me malady can strike both men and women, but women seem more vulnerable because we're encouraged to put others before ourselves. How many of us had mothers who set good examples in self-care?

Women also fall into the trap of believing that if we meet the needs of others, they also will take equally good care of us. Not only does this set us up for disappointment, but it reinforces the notion that we don't really deserve to be comforted.

So what's the solution?

The answer lies in several stages:

1. Believing that self-care is essential and that we deserve it
2. Understanding the harm we cause ourselves (and others) when we don't nurture ourselves
3. Distinguishing when we're sorely in need of self-care
4. Making (not finding) the time
5. Discovering what it is we want and need
6. Doing it

And we just might tack on not feeling guilty about it.

In talks and workshops on nurturing ourselves, I ask participants to make a list of the week's activities under three headings:

1. Like (perhaps walking the dog, aerobics)
2. Dislike (cleaning house, carpooling)
3. Ambivalent (watching TV, chatting on the phone)

Then we discuss giving up, delegating, or sharing those activities we dislike or feel ambivalent about. Maybe we can pay for cleaning or have the family do their share, take the bus instead of carpooling, watch less TV, and limit phone calls to five minutes.

The same type of list will work for people you regularly deal with. The purpose of these exercises is to determine how much time and effort we spend on activities and people that we don't really enjoy— which can mean more time for ourselves.

To get in touch with what we want, we can make an "I love . . ." list in a journal (bubble baths, walks in the woods, popcorn at the movies, long dinners with a friend, etc.). Or "Someday I'll . . ." (backpack through Europe, try my hand at watercolors, etc.). Don't make judgments about your preferences, just jot them down as they occur to you. This helps us know what we enjoy, and it offers us ideas.

Purposely setting aside time for ourselves is important—say, a half hour daily, one evening a week, a weekend day, or an entire weekend each month. Those who share our time may complain, but we can make it clear that this time isn't meant to escape them but to get closer to ourselves.

Mark your "Me Time" on your calendar, and honor that commitment to yourself.

THE ART OF SAYING NO

The slogan "Just say no" seems simple. But why is it so hard to follow?

Lots of us can say no to drugs—but not to carting off to school a kid who's overslept. Or to a frantic boss whose perpetual poor planning becomes our emergency. Or to a lover who feels easily rejected.

Saying no isn't easy—especially for people-pleasers (who feel good about ourselves only if everyone likes us) and for people without personal boundaries (who are unable to set limits for ourselves and others). Saying no is often harder for women than it is for men, as women are trained to placate others and help things go smoothly.

The problem comes when we, for whatever reason, find ourselves saying yes when we want to say no. We grow resentful. We feel overworked and underappreciated. We become victims and martyrs, feeling that everyone else is in control of our lives but us. We want to blame it all on our kids, parents, mates, co-workers. But the truth is, most of us do not have monsters for kids, parents, mates, or co-workers. They are simply human beings who will push where it's possible.

When we can't say no, pushing our boundaries—and our buttons—is easy and even tempting.

It's not a matter of what others try to do to us but of what we allow them to do to us. We have more control over this than we think.

But first it's necessary to understand why we never say no. Basically, we want others to like us. There's nothing wrong with that. But when we're saying yes to the extent that we don't like others or ourselves, we're in deep trouble. We're actually abandoning ourselves so that they won't abandon us.

A word of caution: It gets worse before it gets better (which is often the case with change).

The people to whom we say no may feel hurt, angry, resentful, rejected. They may try to manipulate us into doing what we've just said no to. They'll accuse us of being selfish, not loving them, not being a conscientious employee.

Learning to say no has its stages. At first, we're scared and have to work up our courage to say this simple little word. (It helps to practice on people who don't matter to you—a waiter, a salesperson.) We'll offer a million good reasons to justify our no. Often, we'll give in, just to keep the peace and retain another's approval. Sometimes that two-letter word will generate a long, heated discussion and the whole issue will seem more trouble than it's worth.

To help you say no, try these tricks:

- Identify that feeling of no in your stomach before your mouth says yes.
- Say, "I have to check my calendar and get back to you on that."
- After you're sure you want to decline, call back and say, "I have another commitment then—sorry." That commitment may be to staying in your robe all day, but that's OK.
- Don't be flattered into saying yes. Turn that flattery around: "I have confidence in your being able to handle it well." Remember,

when we insist on doing everything ourselves, we're depriving others of an opportunity to grow.

Eventually, we're able to say no, stick by it, feel good about standing up for ourselves—and stop resenting others. We not only send out the message that we're no longer doormats, but we provide healthy role models for others. (Console yourself with this when your child is telling you what a failure you are as a parent.)

And we'll understand that "No" is a complete sentence—one that greatly simplifies our lives.

MEDITATION, VISUALIZATION, AFFIRMATIONS

Many excellent books are available on meditation, visualization, and affirmations, so we needn't go into detail here other than to stress the importance of having a regular spiritual practice.

If prayer is talking to God, then meditation is listening to God. Both provide a peace which goes beyond the intellect.

Meditation is not retreating from the world but going inside ourselves to learn better how to contribute to our world and its people. It's a process of clearing our minds so that the inner voice (God, intuition, our higher self) may be heard.

Additionally, regular meditation reduces stress, relieves pain, helps control sickness, and fosters spiritual awareness. And it's free!

Visualizing peaceful places and states of mind is an effective way to reduce stress. And visualizing or "imagining" what you want to create in your life is a method that thousands of people swear by.

Chantall Van Wey is a former newspaper copy editor now living her dream of owning a new-and-used bookstore in a magical little town on the Pacific Coast. She realized that dream by practicing creative visualization, and she talks about it so freely that customers demanded to know more.

Chantall found herself explaining the process so much that she decided to put it into written form in a booklet she calls *Chantall's Handy-Dandy Do-It-Yourself Visualization Kit*. She also does seminars on the subject.

Here's what she advises:

Step One: Make a list of the four or five most important things you want manifested in your life.

Step Two: Set aside fifteen minutes in the morning and fifteen minutes at night or fifteen minutes at two intervals during the day when you can be alone and concentrate without distractions. (She sometimes does hers in the shower or tub.)

Step Three: Get into a comfortable position, sit still, and take a few deep breaths to release tension. (If her mind is whirling, she imagines a lake frothy with wind-whipped whitecaps, then imagines it becoming more and more still until it's perfectly placid.)

Step Four: Ask the Universal Source of Abundance and Good to supply you with the things on the list. Include the phrase: "With no harm to myself or anyone else and in Divine Order and the highest good for all concerned."

Chantall stresses the importance during this process of seeing yourself in the act of doing, having, or enjoying whatever you are visualizing to happen or manifest. Feel the joy of ownership or freedom or whatever is your heart's desire.

Don't give up until you've visualized the same list of items, twice a day, for thirty days.

Chantall concedes that it takes work, "but think about what the payoff is. What would you be doing with thirty minutes a day that is more important than altering your life and learning a new skill that will forever change how you feel about yourself and the Universe?"

She cautions visualizers:

- Tell no one what you're doing, lest you weaken the energy.
- Never try to impose your will on someone else.
- And most important of all, believe!

"It is the Universe's good pleasure to fill your life with joy, harmony, love, and abundant prosperity," Chantall firmly believes.

The use of affirmations—short, positive statements regularly repeated—is an effective way of overriding the many negative voices we carry in our heads or are bombarded with from others. Write your own, or consult your library or bookstore for affirmation collections. Many meditation and affirmation books are specifically geared to people in certain situations.

Sweet Silence

As wise Mother Teresa says, "We need to find God, and he cannot be found in noise and restlessness. God is the friend of silence."

If silence is indeed golden, why is there so little of it today?

Daily, we're bombarded by ringing alarms. Morning newscasts on TV or radio. Muzak in elevators and on the phone when we're holding and in grocery stores and shopping malls. Other motorists blasting radios.

And factor in ringing phones, shrieking car alarms (what *is* one supposed to do when a car alarm goes off—accost whoever's closest?), barking dogs, rumbling traffic, and loud commercials and blathering television which stays on nearly twenty-four hours a day in some homes even though no one is watching.

And just watch someone blurt out anything in a group if conversation falls flat for a few seconds.

It's almost as if we fear silence. Our society acts as if silence were a sin.

Why? Because then we might hear the little voice inside that we work so hard to ignore. We might be faced with painful or uncomfortable feelings. We might say something which really matters instead of making endless chitchat.

In the silence, we can hear birds singing. Children laughing. Insects buzzing. Cats purring and dogs barking. Our hearts beating. The words which go unsaid.

And most of all, we can hear our souls singing.

The next time you're tempted to turn on the TV or radio "just for the company," stop.

Savor the silence instead. See what tune your soul is humming these days.

And sing along.

By now, you may be thinking: Solitude is what I have too darned much of!

There's nothing like being single and spending Saturday night alone at home to make you feel sorry for yourself. Sunday afternoon is another poor-little-me equal-opportunity time.

A University of Michigan study shows that social isolation is potentially as dangerous as smoking, high blood pressure, and cholesterol, obesity, or lack of exercise. We need pleasurable contact with others just as much as we need to be alone at times.

Life's too short to be lonely and miserable, a friend and I decided over pasta one Saturday night before seeing a play. We mulled over the typical excuses:

- "Everyone else is probably busy" (the everybody's-at-the-party-but-me syndrome). Ha! Someone would be flattered with your invitation. You just need to keep calling till you find them.
- "I don't want to go alone." Remedy: Buy season tickets to a concert or lecture series or sports event, forcing yourself to invite someone each time.
- "I shouldn't always have to do all the calling." OK, sit there and wait for Prince or Princess Charming! Remember that each person is responsible for his or her own happiness.

Just make a list of activities you might enjoy, make another list of potential people to ask along, then watch the paper for upcoming events and mark your calendar.

Here are some options for future weekends to share or savor alone.

SCORE SOME CULTURE

Trying something new helps you discover new aspects of yourself—and offers opportunities to meet others.

Consider the symphony (classics or pops), holiday programs, ballet, live theater, foreign movies, touring road shows, travelogues, celebrity-speaker series, or comedy clubs.

Don't forget museums (including both art and historical museums tucked away in county seats and small towns), art galleries, weekend produce and crafts markets, flea markets, community festivals, free lectures at bookstores and hospitals, or college and high school theater and musical productions.

SHOP TILL YOU DROP

Instead of heading for the nearest mall, use a little more imagination.

Scope out interesting neighborhood shopping areas; pick up area shopping guides and maps.

Check the phone book for shops catering to special interests—pets, antiques, used books, miniatures, vintage clothing, fishing, cooking. Some neighborhoods or towns offer lists of shops specializing in antiques or used books; check in specific stores or with the chamber of commerce.

Don't forget garage sales, flea markets, holiday gift shows and bazaars, school rummage sales, and factory outlets.

Venture Forth

Make a destination drive. Head for a place you've been before, stopping to do whatever interests you. Or close your eyes and stab at the map; go wherever your finger leads!

Or veer off the beaten path en route to a usual place and discover small towns, interesting shops, scenic spots, historical points of interest. Don't want to drive? Hop a train, bus, city tour, ferry boat ride, or commuter train. Or invite a pal with a car to go along; offer to pay for gas.

Forage for Food

No reason to sit alone trying to get excited about a microwave meal.

Instead, try a new ethnic restaurant, a place that's just opened, a winery tour or wine tasting, a community- or church-sponsored supper.

Go on a quest for the town's best latte, burger, bagel, milkshake, ice cream, burrito, French toast, or whatever is your passion.

Start a tradition of Sunday brunch, Saturday lunch, afternoon tea, Wednesday night pizza, or Friday night dessert.

Shop for fresh produce at the local farmer's market (many are open spring through fall) or a country produce stand. Scout out the best berry patches.

Learn Something New

It's tough to be bored when learning something new, brushing up an old skill, or helping someone else.

Take a night class through the community college, parks and recreation district, YMCA or YWCA, community or senior center, church or synagogue.

Volunteer your time, talent, and attention. (Check for volunteer opportunities in your local newspaper.)

Get physical. Take a class in weight lifting, dancing, yoga, volleyball. Go swimming, hiking, or skating. Participate in a charity walk/run, or join in one of the popular volksmarches. Sign up for a company softball team or bowling league. Join a gym or health club. Get a walking partner.

Use your imagination, find an equally adventurous pal or two, and weekends will never be boring again!

In *Success Is the Quality of Your Journey*, Jennifer James urges us:

"Slow down your external life, simplify as much as possible. The answers to your questions travel slowly and they must be able to catch up with you."

She also notes that "solitude . . . is wonderful because you want to be with the person you're with: yourself."

Plan your daily getaway now.

7. TUNING IN TOGETHERNESS

Family is the most powerful matrix of our life, the source of character and virtue. Family is incredibly important, mysterious, powerful.
—John Bradshaw

The '80s were a time of fractured families—if not from busy schedules and distant moves, then from adult children identifying and disparaging their parents and their mistakes. Some even "divorced" their parents, refusing contact and moving cross-country to escape them.

As this century draws to a close, the value and lasting impact of family is being rediscovered.

Even the "dysfunctional family" guru of publishing and television, John Bradshaw, has softened his position—although he contends his work was misinterpreted if people actually cast family members from their lives.

In *Family Secrets: What You Don't Know Can Hurt You*, he underscores the importance of family connection. He emphasizes acceptance and "loving your own crooked family with your own crooked heart. The reverence we've had for family is justified."

Bradshaw says: "I was more enamored with family dysfunction, so I focused more on the dysfunctional family. What I feel now is Thomas Moore's sense that life is much more soulful and we can't get it in these categories that I thought as a younger man. The family has a soul, deeper than we can fully understand how it impacts our lives."

Retaining the soul of the family is essential in an era where kids turn to gangs to feel they belong.

In a *Life* magazine article, George Howe Colt pointed out that family bonds "are formed less by moments of celebration and of crisis than by the quiet, undramatic accretion of minutiae—the remark on the way out the door, the chore undone, the unexpected smile."

And, let us add, the time spent together. Just as Mormons celebrate Mondays as Family at Home Night, we can rethink some of our commitments and create time for what's truly important.

And family *is* important.

WORKAHOLISM KILLS RELATIONSHIPS

Riddle: What's the best way to please your boss and frustrate your mate?

Answer: Work overtime. Bring work home. Break promises to the family when work interrupts plans.

As we push to succeed, relationships suffer, sometimes even die. Yet the pressure is greater than ever to spend more time on the job.

A survey of 3,000 male readers by a business magazine shows: More than half work more than sixty hours weekly; 29 percent more than seventy hours. More than half fight about it with their wives at least monthly, almost 25 percent at least once weekly. One-third bring work home and work till 11 p.m. or midnight; some work eighty hours a week and don't get to bed until 2 a.m.

Who has time—or energy—for love?

Now, we're not talking here about a healthy work ethic, company loyalty, or job integrity. We're talking about buying the myth that working long hours to the exclusion of having a life is good for you.

It isn't.

Look at the myths:

Hard work brings company gratitude. Not necessarily. Ask those whose company has been laying people off. Ask workers in a firm taken over by another corporation or by new managers. What you've accomplished can count for nothing overnight. No one is indispensable.

Working long hours proves you love your family. Have you asked your mate or kids lately how they feel about your perpetual physical or emotional absence? Do you find yourself offering your family things instead of time? Two-thirds of the men working eighty or more hours weekly said in the magazine survey that they appeased their families by buying expensive gifts or sending them off on fancy vacations.

Working overtime shows you're successful. Not necessarily. It may just indicate you're a workaholic, confusing productivity with busyness, and leisure with wasting time. Worst of all, workaholics confuse work with personal worth. These are the people who ignore family and friends, who feel worthless upon retiring, who die soon after retirement—or make their mates so miserable they wish they would die.

Hard work gets you into heaven. That's what theologian John Calvin would have us believe. These days, it gets you burnout.

So how we can prevent job burnout and family alienation?

Bookstores and libraries are full of books on job stress. Some counselors specialize in the subject. We can avail ourselves of all these.

We can get our priorities straight—like the man who told me, "I promised myself I wouldn't turn fifty and realize I didn't know my kids." We can turn down promotions. Learn to work more efficiently. Leave when the workday is over instead of waiting for the boss's light to go out. Stop carrying work home.

We can stop buying into the myths that are easily exploded by those who've been riffed, "downsized," or encouraged to retire ahead of us. Remember the lie carved over the gates of the Nazi concentration camps: "Work shall make you free."

Working long and hard may make you the workplace pet. It may make you rich or even famous. It may make you CEO.

But it won't make you popular with those you love most. And those are the folks who matter.

CREATING TIME TOGETHER

Time together won't happen automatically; we have to make it happen. And if it's truly important to us, we do just that. We set time aside for those we love—first.

- Schedule time with your partner or kids or parents regularly. Write it on the calendar in red.

- Decide what works best for you: A date every Friday night? A walk together after dinner? A leisurely breakfast Saturday mornings? Discuss it with those involved.

- Plan as many meals together as possible; establish some as mandatory. Preparing the meal, serving it attractively, enjoying it, and even cleaning up can become an unhurried ritual providing cherished time together.

- Make a date with a child. Each child gets special time alone with Mom or Dad on a regular basis. It may just be a burger out, but it's undivided attention. One dad takes each child out for a special dinner alone with him near their birthdays.

- Get away alone as a couple, without the kids. Do this partnership right, and it will endure long after the children are gone. Money tight? Arrange to bunk the kids with Gramma or a friend; sleep naked, enjoy breakfast in bed, be romantic. Take your turn keeping the friend's children to return the favor.

- Make family get-togethers special by keeping the TV off and using your imagination. Get out the board games. Show the kids what you used to do as kids. Tell family stories. Get up a ball game in the backyard or nearby park. After a family dinner at my house recently, three generations played charades of sorts—complete with impromptu costumes. We divided into teams of two adults and one child, then suggested or let the kids decide what story they wanted to act out. Grampa, Daddy, and Zach draped towels around their shoulders to become dueling Three Musketeers. Brittany, Aunt, and Uncle did Little Red Riding Hood. Confined to the couch with a bad back, Mom was the slumbering Snow White, three-year-old Ashley a weeping dwarf, and Gramma the Prince Charming who awoke her. We not only played and laughed together, but the kids didn't want to quit.

- Consider family camping trips. Several families I know get together every Labor Day weekend at a campground, expanding the number of tents to cover the growing numbers of grandchildren.

FAMILY MEETINGS

It used to be that families sat down together for daily dinners. The meal provided an automatic setting for discussing each person's day, planning the upcoming family vacation, or explaining the need to cut expenditures for a while.

More and more, that opportunity for such discussion needs to be created. That's why some families turn to regularly scheduled family meetings. This works for both two-parent and single-parent families.

Family meetings can be of three basic types:

BUSINESS

During the meeting, anyone can say anything (politely) without reprisal. This is a time to listen and not interrupt, to truly hear what each family member is saying without leaping in with advice, warnings, or judgments.

For successful meetings, use these guidelines and adjust them to fit your needs:

- Hold meetings to an hour.
- Include everyone living in the household.
- Post a discussion agenda ahead of time.
- Begin or end with a circle of compliments: everyone says something they've appreciated about each person during the past week.
- Give each person uninterrupted time to air problems, gripes, or concerns.
- Encourage "I" messages: "I feel upset when people come into my room without asking" rather than "Tommy always barges in on me."
- Understand that parents have the final say-so.
- Conclude with a treat, such as popcorn, an ice-cream cone out, a trip to the park.

RECREATIONAL OR EDUCATIONAL

The purpose of these meetings is simply constructive togetherness. You may want to choose a theme for each session, such as peace, ecology, money, kindness. And plan activities, such as watching and analyzing a TV show, learning about a famous person, cooking an ethnic meal for a country you've studied together.

An excellent guide for such times is *Just Family Nights: Sixty Activities to Keep Your Family Together in a World Falling Apart*, edited by Susan Vogt.

SPIRITUAL

Janet Luhrs is a single mother of two and founder of the quarterly *Simple Living* journal (see Resources). Each Sunday evening after dinner, she and her children gather on pillows in front of the fireplace. They turn the lights down and light a family candle. They discuss the good things that happened that week as well as problems and solutions. They select a virtue to work on for the week. Then they sing or read something spiritual.

"The kids love this quiet, special time together," Janet reports. "This has been a new lesson for me; you can't just try to fit this kind of thing into your life when it is convenient—you need to MAKE and KEEP the time."

COPING WITH STEPFAMILIES

Jerry and Lynn are crazy about each other and hope to marry. She loves the way he's so caring. He adores her big heart.

They've been living together eight months. Or trying to. Lynn is on the verge of moving out because she's so frustrated with his sixteen-year-old daughter.

Lynn and Jerry aren't their true names, but they are a real couple facing the problems common to those who remarry. From 60 to 70 percent of second marriages end in divorce.

Lynn, thirty-five, says: "I love him with all my heart, but my therapist has said, move or go on medication. When his daughter came to live with us, Jerry and she made all the arrangements without talking to me. She lies, she's wrecked the car, she's slept with her boyfriend in my bed. He's so naive. He turns his back and makes it all me—I'm always the bad guy. He's letting the child control us, setting limits but not following through. I feel resentful and abandoned."

Jerry, forty-three, says: "I love both of them. I enjoy a wonderful relationship with my daughter and wish Lynn could be friends with her. She's a good kid. I know I'm too passive. In my marriage, her mother handled the discipline. Lynn and I have been in counseling, and I've stepped up to bat at my responsibilities as a parent. I don't think all our relationship issues can be put on the shoulders of the child. I don't want Lynn to move, but I can't abandon my daughter."

We bring wisdom and experience to subsequent relationships, and many of us also bring children. That means responsibilities, loyalties, and concerns that aren't a part of first unions.

Not to mention emotional baggage—the parental guilt of having divorced in the first place or perhaps even of having left our child physically. The circumstances of the departure (another party involved, a custody battle) often make matters worse.

When one or more children live with us and our new love, home can feel like a fireworks factory in the heat of summer.

If the kid is our child, we may feel eager to make up for past transgressions, unable to discipline or say no and be consistent about it, anxious to look better than the other parent, afraid we'll slight either our child or our partner, or so eager to please both that we're often walking a tightrope.

Sometimes we just wish that both of them would disappear!

If the kid is our partner's, we might feel jealous of their shared history and the fact that he or she loved someone else before us, resentful of the intrusion and having to share our partner, fearful of not being a perfect stepparent, sure our partner is handling the situation wrong, concerned that the child is getting more attention and time than we are or that our own children are, or convinced that our partner always sides with the child against us.

And it's so easy to see how our partner is being manipulated by his or her child. Yet it's never so obvious when our own kid is manuevering us.

Here's what the experts on stepparenting advise:

- Let the child's own parent be the disciplinarian at first. Don't make your partner the heavy, but make it clear to your child that the partner is in charge when you're not around. A new partner should act as a child's friend and confidant rather than parent at first.
- Make it clear to your child that your partner must be treated with respect: Don't allow your child to treat the adult you love rudely. Your partner's feelings are as important as your child's.
- Discuss family rules together so that everyone understands them: Agree on the rules; post them and be consistent in enforcing them. Family meetings are a good way to let everyone vent feelings safely.
- Make time alone with your partner as well as with your stepchild: Focus on your relationship by taking time out from the children's demands; stave off triangular disputes by encouraging your partner and child to get to know and appreciate each other as individuals.
- Learn more about stepparenting. Help is available from the Stepfamily Association of America, Inc. (See Resources.)

STAYING CONNECTED LONG-DISTANCE

Having children sometimes makes us wonder if we have a hole in our heads.

But when divorce or family moves take our children or grandchildren from us, it can leave a definite hole in our hearts: no more spur-of-the-moment overnights, every-other-weekend visits, popping by to pick up a child to go for ice cream.

But there are ways to stay in loving contact through the miles with beloved youngsters:

- Write frequently. Children love getting their own mail. Include self-addressed, stamped envelopes to ensure a reply.

- Set up a weekly phone date, say 7 p.m. each Sunday night. And let them know they can call you collect anytime.

- Encourage them to send drawings, schoolwork, and copies of report cards to decorate your fridge. Send them a photo of you with their displayed artwork.

- Send recordings of yourself. Tell stories of your childhood, their childhood, how you felt when they were born. Read or tell a favorite tale; sing lullabies or nonsense songs.

- Share your travels. Send the kids postcards, stamps, decals, seashells, or foreign money from exotic places. Encourage them to start a collection.

- Create a photo album just for them of shared times. Have double prints made of photos whenever you and they are together. One divorced dad assembles an album for his kids at the end of every two-month summer visit.

- Tuck items of interest into your letters. Try stickers, sports cards, pictures, newspaper or magazine articles.

- Videotape yourself giving a guided tour. Tour your home or town, perhaps the child's former neighborhood if they have moved, the hospital where they were born. Stir their memories by asking questions as you go along: "Here is the house you used to live in. Do you remember what color it was before the new people painted it? Do you remember where Gramma keeps the toys? Let's look there and see if you are right. Here is the birdhouse you helped hang. Can you recall how many baby birds we had last summer?"
- Have old photos copied and make a family album for them. Include your grandparents, parents, yourself, your children, and your grand-children to give them a sense of where they came from. Write bits of history, favorite family stories, and similarities you see in the child and other relatives.
- Videotape your favorite family photos. The kids can pop the "album" into the VCR for easy viewing.
- Send significant children's books. Buy those about parents and grandparents, experiences and places you've enjoyed together, books that relate to the children's interests or circumstances.
- Keep a journal for each child. Write your feelings about them, funny things they say in person or over the phone, what you experienced at their ages, and so on.
- Make a special gift that will be a link with you, such as a chair, comforter, doll or stuffed animal, shelf, or birdhouse.
- Plan a trip you will make together. Send travel brochures, post-cards, ideas, and let them help with the decision-making. If they'll

be entertaining you, ask them to make a list of must-sees they want to show you.

Many of these things will make lovely family keepsakes long after we are gone.

And remember, it may be difficult to be far away from those precious little people, but long-distance is better than no children or grand-children at all!

PARENTS OF TEENS, HANG IN THERE

Parents of teenagers, take heart! There is affection after adolescence. Even friendship.

For those of you who'd like to deep-freeze your teen till twenty-one—you're not alone. It's a toss-up whether puberty is tougher on the kids or the parents. And if you're a single parent, you have no ally against the enemy.

It seems to happen overnight. Your cherished children, your enthu-siastic little buddies who want to be just like you when they grow up, go to bed one evening and wake up as a tabloid headline: ADOLESCENT TURNS ALIEN IN SLEEP!

Where is the little person you bundled home from the hospital? The tearful tot who clung to you that first day of kindergarten?

Gone for nearly a decade, that's where.

Teens don't look up to you unless you're on a ladder—holding your wallet. You only tower in the eyes of their friends: "Your mom is like, so rad! I wish we could trade." Your child rolls her eyes.

Parenting a teen can drive you to drink—if the little darling doesn't beat you to the bottle first. I raised three teenagers, all in their twenties now and people of whom I'm proud—people I even like, who think of me as their friend.

It wasn't always so.

I learned—the hard way—that this is what teenagers need:

To know we're there. They may say they don't need us at all, but they do. They need to know we want to be with them, that we're available to talk, that we're willing to put their needs above our own much of the time.

To be different from us. Whether it's politics, clothes, music, religion, or whatever, it's part of them proving to themselves who they are, separate from us. Don't take it personally or overreact.

To be loved, even when they're not lovable. When children act up, that's when they need us most. We can say, "I love you," cite their attributes, touch them as they pass, check up on where they're going (even if they protest), and not give up on them.

To be heard. Their ideas may seem naive, dangerous, or heretical, but adolescence means exploration. One of our jobs is to help them become good thinkers. "That's one way of looking at it. Have you thought about . . . ?" is a more constructive response than "That's the most idiotic idea I've ever heard!" Make a habit of asking their opinions about family decisions, current events, ethical issues, and so on.

To hear our own stories of the pain of growing up. There's a difference between sharing our experience and preaching. If we suspect they're having a specific problem, it feels less attacking to say, "Did I ever tell you about the time I . . . ?" instead of launching into advice-giving or trying to draw them out. Hearing their grandparents' version of our teen years can offer them perspective as well—and prove we really were young once.

To belong. Create time together, even if they bring a friend along. Including them in extended family gatherings will help them see they're part of something larger than a one- or two-parent family—and they may find a relative they can talk with easily. Expose them to family history, share family stories.

To have a spiritual base. This may come from church or synagogue attendance (teen groups can provide positive peer support) or volunteer work you do as a family (such as serving meals to the homeless).

Remember: You will survive. Your beloved child, who's such a pain right now, eventually will become your friend. Hang in there.

As Dad used to say, "This, too, shall pass."

VACATIONS WHICH UNIFY

Ah, the delicious anticipation of planning your vacation! You and your partner nestle on the couch, surrounded by travel brochures, maps, and guidebooks. You agree on where, what, and when. You call a travel agent and pull out your charge card—nothing to do now but plan what to pack and look forward to the memories you'll make.

What's wrong with this picture?

People can love each other dearly, even agreeing on politics and movies—but not on vacations.

Don and Stacy can't. The fifty-six-year-old lawyer and thirty-six-year-old social worker are engaged—and disagreeing about their first major vacation together.

Her plan is to take the red-eye flight to Florida and explore Disney World for four days from 6 a.m. to late-night closing. She's gotten guidebooks, studied them for months, and worked out her strategy for seeing the most in the most efficient way. If Stacy misses anything she wants to see, she feels cheated.

Don is the opposite. He's content to stroll hand-in-hand and watch people. Stacy suggested that he park himself on a bench and meet her at an appointed time, but that feels like too much structure and too little time together.

How do they solve the dilemma?

Lively or laid-back, there is no "right" way to vacation. But couples whose traveling styles don't jibe are likely to wind up frustrated, feuding, and maybe even finished if they don't acknowledge and accommodate their different vacation expectations.

You want to bring back souvenirs, photos, and warm memories—not resentments.

If you're vacationing as a couple (or even with a friend), here are some suggestions for planning and enjoying time together you'll both savor.

BEFORE YOUR VACATION

Assess what you want and expect from a vacation. Ask yourself: What does vacation mean to me? How do I want to feel during and after? Do

I need stimulation (new people, interesting places, unusual food) or respite from the world (no phone and TV, isolation)? Do I want to spend every moment with my partner, or do I need time alone? What have I always wanted to see or do?

Discuss what each of you wants and arrange to get some of both. There's no reason you can't divide your trip into sections: city and rural, scheduled and unplanned, sightseeing and lounging.

Consider staying home and doing nothing. You don't have to range far afield and go into debt in order to have quality time together and truly relax. Follow the suggestions above; free each other from regular chores and routines; and don't plan a project that will make vacation time into work. Make day trips, try new restaurants, sleep in, have friends over.

Divide travel tasks. It's easy to wrestle for control, especially if you're used to traveling alone. Agree ahead of time who will carry tickets or travel documents, handle bags, collect brochures, call cabs, make reservations, and so on. You can also alternate travel tasks.

Limit luggage if you'll be on the go. Keep it to what you can tote for several blocks. Remember the traveler's axiom: Take half the clothes you think you'll need—and twice as much money!

DURING YOUR VACATION

Plan for time alone. Go your separate ways for the morning or afternoon, then reunite over lunch or dinner. It's no fun shopping, museum-browsing, or horseback riding with a reluctant companion. Parents can take turns with the kids.

Make sure each day offers a treat for each person. Compromising on shared activities will be easier if you plan at least one thing each of you really wants to do that day—be it breakfast in bed or a vigorous hike.

Alternate activity and sightseeing with leisure. Tour the amusement park or the museum in the morning; then enjoy a long lunch or relax on the beach. Both adults and kids need a break. Overscheduling—even with fun—can feel too much like work. It's your vacation; you don't have to see and do everything in the guide book.

Celebrate your love. Vacationing together can help you grow closer. Bringing work along, keeping a frenetic pace, or catering only to the kids can be a way of staving off intimacy.

Not all vacations need to be in tandem. Many couples enjoy going off to do their own thing: he goes on an archaeological dig, she visits relatives; he plays golf, she hikes with friends. You may feel a stronger sense of self and have a new appreciation of each other when you get back together.

Don and Stacy have decided that she'll go to Disney World with a girlfriend willing to try to keep pace. When she returns, Stacy and Don will drive to Montana together.

"She gets in at 10 p.m. and wants me to pick her up at the airport, and we'll go on from there," Don says with a sigh. At least he'll be rested.

HOLD A FAMILY REUNION

Family is a chain from the past into the future; reunions provide not only context but also connection.

How long has it been since you've seen that cousin you teased as a kid? Ever wished you knew more about your family history? Would you like your children to see Gramma just once more before you become the oldest generation? You may be ready for a family reunion.

Yours can be formal or free-form as family size and desire dictate, but such a gathering requires planning and leadership. Now's the time to start work on a family reunion for next year.

Here are some suggestions from reunion experts.

SURVEY THE FAMILY

If you're considering a first reunion, send a written survey to all known family members. Questions to include: Would they come? How far are they willing to travel? What dates are most convenient? What activities do they like? Are they willing to help plan? Who can help locate lost relatives? Who can donate equipment or talents? As plans progress, often more people volunteer their time and skills.

SET THE DATE AND LOCATION

Summer is the most common time for reunions because it's easier for families to travel. Plan outdoor activities. Holidays may be better for those in school or in the military. If the family is far-flung and your reunions are regular, consider moving the location around the country each year and make it a vacation destination. Setting the date a year in advance allows for planning and ensures greater attendance.

Reunion locations range from a member's home or restaurant banquet room for a small gathering to a rented vacation home, park, hall, campground, resort, convention center, or even a cruise ship for a larger group (some cruise lines offer discounts).

Send Invitations

The more thorough the information on the invitation, the better. Consider using a business-conference brochure as a sample. Include a map and list of events along with times and locations, costs, information on lodging, and the number to call for reservations. At the bottom, print a reunion registration form, including a mailing address for its return, space for names of each member of the individual family attending, and line items to fill in, such as: Registration/activity reservations for __ at $2 each=$__; Dinner reservations for __ adults at $19 each= $__; Dinner reservations for __ children at $12 each=$__. Include a deadline to ensure a prompt reply. You may want to include a list of local attractions which people can plan vacations around. And don't forget lists of RV and motel accommodations so that people can book their own reservations.

For smaller groups, forgo formal invitations and keep each other posted with bulletins.

Establish a Budget

Like weddings, family reunions have a way of mushrooming. Unless you have a rich relative who's willing to underwrite the gathering, you'll likely have to charge a fee to cover such expenses as postage, printing, hall rental, portable toilets, food, and decorations. It makes sense to plan the reunion the way conferences are planned: Tally your expenses, divide the total by the number of people expected to attend, then set a registration fee. If you run short, you can pass the hat.

Cut costs by having attendees pay for their motel rooms, buy their own meals, and bring food to communal meals.

DELEGATE DUTIES

An effective reunion demands thorough planning, and most reunions are more than a one-person job.

Some families appoint a director and assistant director to plan the next event. The director sets the date and updates family members with newsletters. Some appoint a historian to assemble a family tree and history and to coordinate old photos and mementos. If your reunion is large, you may want to set aside a special room as a "family museum."

PLAN THE FOOD

A potluck with everyone contributing is the easiest way to handle a one-meal reunion. Even easier is having your reunion catered, but the cost could become prohibitive over several days. A one- or two-day meeting at a hotel could include cost of hotel meals.

For longer reunions, some families appoint meal committees of local people who can easily prepare food, supplying extra quantity for those who are traveling and can't cook. Or put each immediate family in charge of a different meal. They can plan the menu, supply the food, and prepare it. Some meals can be bring-your-own.

STRUCTURE ACTIVITIES

Talking is the most important part of any family reunion, but it shouldn't be the only thing going on. To liven things up, stage informal softball and volleyball games. Hold a Family Olympics. Schedule horseshoes, chess, checkers, or Trivial Pursuit tournaments. Stage a talent show, skit, sing-along, square dance (with lessons), or cooking contest.

Some reunions include church services. (One family called in a priest to say Mass for them on the motel lawn.) Others take a stroll through the cemetery where ancestors are buried, watch videos of trips made to the old country, tour the old homestead, or hold a program featuring family history and anecdotes along with a slide show of old photographs.

One large Oregon family began its reunion with a Friday night reception in the memorabilia room, which included a copy machine and computers for accessing the 500-entry family tree. A registration packet included maps of the area with family property marked as well as directions to the Oregon Trail for those who wanted to see the wagon-wheel ruts their ancestors helped dig.

Families who meet regularly often hold a family meeting to announce marriages and births and to memorialize those who have died. The official group photo may be taken at this time and officers elected or committees appointed for the next reunion.

And don't forget kids and teens.

Team sports, swimming, races and games, face-painting, perhaps a clown or magician, and a teen dance will happily occupy the younger set. A very large reunion could feature a kiddy room with videos and childcare during special adult programs.

Offer Keepsakes

These may be a family directory, a copy of the family tree, a family history, a group photo, a videotape, a cookbook to which everyone has contributed recipes, and coffee or beer mugs, key chains, T-shirts, baseball caps, banners, rubber stamps, or stationery.

Large families which hold regular reunions often have the family name and logo printed on some of these items and sell them. Selling the items at a small profit can help cover reunion costs.

Need to feel connected with family? Hold a reunion.

In the words of songwriter Don Eaton, "That's why we keep on loving, that's how we get back home."

8. HONORING OUR ANCESTORS

We all grow up with the weight of history on us. Our ancestors dwell in the attics of our brains as they do in the spiraling chains of knowledge hidden in every cell of our bodies.
—Shirley Abbott, *Womenfolks: Growing Up Down South*

We are more than individuals or members of our immediate families. We each are links in an endless human chain we call family.

In our increasingly isolated society, it's essential that both adults and children—especially children—understand that they are part of something larger than the household in which they live. Knowing this offers them options, security, role models, history, and a taste of immortality.

Ours is a society of families living far apart, of divorce and remarriage and divorce yet again. It's impossible to keep track of family members without a program.

This program, however, is at our fingertips. Computers enable us not only to build our family trees but to research information on the web.

For better or for worse, family does impact us, not just in childhood but through the generations.

Let's look at how we can connect with those who came before us.

FAMILY PHOTOS

When home tragedies strike and families are forced to flee fires, floods, and hurricanes, the one thing they most regret losing is irreplaceable family photos.

Photos—and increasingly, videotapes—are a legacy we enjoy, learn from, and pass on. They are proof of youth, the progress of aging, the validation of life lived long. Photos show us that we are truly connected, perhaps with family we've never met. See that nose and hairline on my father at twenty—the picture of my son at the same age, isn't it?

Here are some ways to organize, preserve, enjoy, and even heal old wounds with your family photographs.

GETTING CAUGHT UP

Do you know what it's like to haul a monster around on your shoulders for twenty-five years? We all have 'em.

Your monster may be those wedding thank-you's you've never written. Or the neighbor's power tool you borrowed and broke and hope he doesn't remember whom he lent it to. My monster is that I was twenty-five years behind on my photo albums.

I got behind, you see, because I have three kids, and then one of those kids popped out three new little people before I ever dreamed of becoming a grandmother. Plus, I travel a lot. And I love to take pictures.

The result was a kitchen countertop littered with envelopes of photos. Drawers crammed full. Boxes stacked in the closet. And even bookshelves lined with old albums which were falling apart and in need of reorganization.

I couldn't get started—true to perfectionist form—because I had to do it perfectly. Sound familiar?

Yuck! It was easier not to start, to just make friends with my monster.

Then I heard a talk on organizing photos. The speaker stressed what a legacy labeled photo albums are for our children and all those who come after.

She got me motivated, and I realized I had to start. Anywhere. Any project starts with one small step.

So I bought a pretty box complete with organizer cards. (A shoebox with index cards would do.) In pencil, I labeled the dividers TRAVELS, MY KIDS, BIRTHDAYS, HOLIDAYS, FRIENDS AND RELATIVES, ME, and GRANDKIDS.

Then I tackled the teetering pile on the counter, sticking them into the proper places.

By the end of the evening, my box was full and two surfaces were cleared. I became nearly hysterical with relief, just like my daughter did when she was small and she survived a doctor's visit without a shot.

Next—at my leisure, because the mess and guilt aren't in my face—I'll get a few more boxes so that each child and grandchild has his or her own. The subdivisions will be more specific: BIRTH, BABYHOOD, CHILD-HOOD, TEENS, ADULTHOOD, WORKING, and so on. As I sort, I'll pull out the best shots of each person and use them to make a collage to frame and display.

Even if I never get around to putting the photos in albums, now I can get at any photo I need or pull out a section to share with others. The kids can easily retrieve their "archives" when I'm gone.

And best of all, I've said goodbye to that monster I've known for twenty-five years. Too bad I forgot to take his picture.

Keeping Photos Safe

We can damage pictures unwittingly—even without a fire—by improper care of photos and and negatives.

Here's how to protect this precious legacy:

- Store negatives apart from photos. If one is damaged, you'll have the other.
- Keep negatives by the roll in an envelope, with date and subject noted. For absolute safety, store them in a fireproof box—or at least where the temperatures are not very hot or very cold.
- Don't feel compelled to keep every snapshot—just the best ones. Professional photographers shoot away, knowing they'll get several good ones off each roll. Be discriminating.
- Use photo-safe albums and scrapbooks made from paper that is free of damaging acid.
- Date and name each person on or near the photo (but not in ball-point pen) to avoid those "mystery shots" we've all inherited.

Displaying Photos

After all the work of organizing photos, this is the fun part. There are several ways to do it:

Albums. I'll never forget the pain of tearing apart Mom's carefully-assembled family photo albums after she died and we five siblings took back pictures of our childhoods and our children. Avoid this by creating your own family album and one for each child. When they leave home, they can take theirs with them.

You may also want to keep a specialty album for birthdays or holidays. I keep a Christmas album (which includes Thanksgiving and New Year's shots), adding photos and my Christmas letter each year. Not a holiday season goes by that the entire family doesn't enjoy looking through it.

Wall displays. The advantage to this is that photos are out where we can enjoy them daily; we don't have to drag out heavy albums. A hallway is a natural photo gallery. Give an entire wall over to it. Some families have a group portrait taken yearly; one mother lines her family room with this pictorial history. Such galleries can be set up in bedrooms as well. You may wish to visually tie photos of the same person together by running a ribbon behind the picture backs.

Collages. These provide a method of displaying lots of pictures in a compact space. Either buy frames precut with several holes in the mat or create your own by simply attaching photos with the edges overlapping (safely and carefully, so they can be unstuck) to a sheet of heavy paper.

Collages may contain shots of everyone or be kept to a single person. Theme collages are fun and are real conversation pieces. My sister Sally displays one of extended family weddings and another of her family's pets over the years. I created collages of my three children and three grandchildren in the process of toilet-training and another of babies and tots in the tub. Soon, I'll compile one of kids in Halloween costumes. You could do various homes you've lived in, cars you've owned, cute baby shots, and so on.

INSPIRING, FORGIVING, AND HEALING WITH PHOTOS

Ever heard of photo therapy?

It's a method some therapists use to help clients deal with unresolved emotions and family issues. We can learn a lot about our childhoods by going through albums and examining the pictures more closely and noting: Who's not in the picture? Who is always touching who? Does someone invariably hold a drink in their hand? Is there a period in which no snapshots were made? What emotions arise as you look at certain photos?

Working with a therapist or alone, we can use family photos to inspire, forgive, and heal.

Is there a grandmother you much admire, one whose qualities you'd like to develop? Give her photo a place of honor, perhaps in your bedroom where you'll see it first thing each morning. What traits did she have—courage, adventure, humor, wisdom—that you want more of? You may want to list those traits on a piece of paper and post it with the picture. Let her inspire you to be the best you can be.

Are you at odds with your father? Select a picture of him—if possible, at a young age, or at least younger than you are now. Place this photo lower than eye level so that you're not looking up to him as a child does to a parent. Can you see the hope in that young face?

Similarities to your own face or personality? How did life hurt him after that photo was taken? Find a picture of him as a child. Can you hold that child mentally and comfort him for the pain he will face? Eventually, the all-powerful parent will become simply a person who—like all of us—did the best with what he had and sometimes blew it. Keep this photo out until you can forgive.

Find a photo of yourself taken during a difficult period in your life—sexual abuse, rejection by a lover, or your parents' divorce. Put that picture in a lovely frame and put it by your bedside—or have a copy made and carry it in your wallet. Tell that person you love her. Tell her why. List her good qualities. Assure her that things will be better. Tell her that the abuse wasn't her fault. Love that younger self, and heal.

FAMILY HISTORIES

Do you remember listening as a child to dreary grown-up talk of relatives you remember only dimly or never even met? How boring it all seemed.

As we age and see our children and grandchildren grow, we understand that we are but a link in the human chain called family. We sense our own mortality and suddenly grasp that we are someone's ancestor. We become curious about those who came before us, just as one day a great-great-nephew might wonder more about us.

Oh, if only we'd listened to the elders tell their tales!

We can't go back, but we can learn more about our families. Genealogy makes a useful and compelling hobby.

FAMILY TREES

Family trees become more and more difficult to record on standard printed forms when there is so much divorce and remarriage. But the complications don't have to keep us from this engrossing task.

There are several ways to go about this:

- Take a genealogy class or read a book on the subject.

- Map out what and who you know in tree form; this is a good visual way to understand the various branches and to see what you already have and what blanks you need to fill. If possible, add a picture of each person next to their name. You may even want to branch out to create a "geneagram" listing behavioral traits, causes of death, and other characteristics along with birth and death dates. This enables you to see how families hand down patterns.

- Contact older relatives for information and photos they have. Offer to copy and return the photos. Ask them about their cousins and other relatives you don't know who also may have information. Ask whether anyone else has compiled a family history. You may be able to save yourself some work.

- Take advantage of the extensive genealogical libraries that Mormons keep. Inquire at a local Church of Jesus Christ of Latter-day Saints.

- Go on-line. By searching through a list of last names, my brother found a distant cousin who'd been searching for information for years. They traded information and even met in person.

Oral Histories

Don't waste another moment. Grab a tape recorder and interview older family members. This is easier for them than trying to write it all down.

Ask specific questions, just as a reporter would. If they live far away, send a list of your questions and invite them to record their memories at leisure. Don't forget to ask questions such as "How did you get to school? What was your first car? How much did you earn at your first real job?" Ask, too, about family scandals and black sheep.

You may also want to ask siblings and other relatives to write their own brief histories or obituaries. This ensures that current family history will be accurately compiled, and it may be of interest to future family historians.

Reunions

No matter where we grew up, whether we have loads in common or would never have picked one another as pals, the family members who we meet at reunions are invariably a gift. We learn different things about ourselves from each one depending on their age, personality, and circumstance.

These gifts include:

Context. Family is more than the group we grew up with; we are also nieces and grandsons and cousins—and eventually great-grandparents. We are descendants of those in fuzzy photographs and will be ancestors to those unseen. We come to understand our parents better—even if they are dead—by hearing an aunt or uncle discuss their childhoods.

The grandparents we knew simply as loving old people become rounded as we hear their life histories unraveled by their now elderly child. Shared anecdotes cast people in a whole new light. What? Prim and proper Aunt Virginia was evicted from a restaurant for starting a food fight?

Recognition of patterns. Alcoholism, sarcasm, bull-headedness? It's hard to blame someone when you see where they got it. Or a great sense of humor, artistic talent, the gift of gab. We see how we become our parents, for better or for worse—and how we can shuck the less-desirable traits if we identify and understand why they didn't work then and won't work now. We may have inherited our way of smiling, but we can correct our tendency for put-downs.

Corrected misconceptions. Because we got boxes of hand-me-downs and were taken out to dinner when well-to-do relatives visited, we felt like the poor, inferior relatives. Comparing childhoods with cousins, we learn how lucky we were in many ways. We understand that all families have problems, some more evident than others. We see the sad, isolating trap of playing "look good."

Continued connection. As we laugh and cry and remember and catch up, those who have gone feel close. Surely they are just in the next room. We who loved them best can offer a toast, knowing that death does not diminish love.

Solved mysteries. There are your son's ears on your uncle! And you learn that your great-grandfather, a doctor, wasn't shot in a cemetery but in his own home office. And yes, that gray-haired lady, Aunt Hazel, was the baby with whom great-grandmother was pregnant when great-grandfather was shot. A reunion's a good time to gather family facts and stories. We all hold a piece of the puzzle called family.

For suggestions about planning a reunion, see Chapter 7, "Tuning in Togetherness."

Here's to family—God bless 'em!

9. THE HAND OF HOSPITALITY

In this world of constant change and rootlessness, we need the solace of friendship perhaps more than ever before.
—Susan Jeffers, *Dare to Connect*

Remember the days when you could make a date with a pal, pronto—without both of you having to leaf ahead two months in your datebooks before finding an opening?

These taxing times make it tough to maintain friendships. With so few hours to handle work, home, and family, how on earth do you fit in friends?

Yet friendship requires nurturing. Though mutual attraction may be spontaneous, maintaining closeness with another requires commitment, time, and effort.

Why bother?

Friends provide support that mates can't always give. They offer a link with the past. They lend a fresh perspective on our lives. They know us—and love us anyway.

In *Dare to Connect: Reaching Out in Romance, Friendship and the Workplace*, Susan Jeffers calls friendship "the safety net of the heart."

Yet many of us avoid the expenditure of energy that making, keeping, and entertaining friends entails.

Some of us grew up in homes where drop-in guests were easily welcomed. Just shove that laundry over and have a seat!

Not so in my family. Things had to be just so, which carried the unfortunate message that we weren't OK unless our home was perfect.

"Company's coming—gotta re-shingle the roof!" became a joke among us grown siblings after we'd analyzed this.

Yet the most memorable company meal of all was the evening Mom dropped the pot of spaghetti on the floor just as our guest walked up the driveway! Mom fled to the bedroom in tears. (She was exhausted from managing five kids and scrubbing the kitchen floor that day.) Dad and we kids just scooped it up and had it on the table by the time the doorbell rang. We didn't tell our guest what had happened until years later.

To this day, I'm one-quarter appalled and three-quarters admiring of a person who doesn't apologize for a home that looks lived in when company comes.

The truth is: People want to be with *us*, not with our perfectly polished table. Wouldn't you rather sit on the floor eating pizza with laughing friends than sit ramrod straight at a formal dinner with companions who bore you silly?

We can feel at ease entertaining and help guests feel welcome by recognizing several principles:

- We are valued for ourselves, not for our possessions.
- Spotless/new/gourmet/expensive has nothing to do with fun, compassion, connection, or intellectual stimulation.
- The more comfortable we feel, the more relaxed our guests will be.
- Being with a few people we genuinely care about is more soul-satisfying than hosting a huge social payback with a crowd of folks who don't really matter to us.
- Graciousness amounts to caring how the people in our home feel and meeting their needs with a giving heart.

To make guests feel welcome, all we really need to do is simply care that they are there.

ENTERTAINING EASILY AND INEXPENSIVELY

Like public speaking, the idea of entertaining friends in our home sparks fear in many of us. What if the party doesn't go perfectly? But I can't afford to serve quality wine. I'm not much of a cook. My furniture's too shabby. Others are so creative and I'm not.

Because of this, some people never ask folks over. But they miss what can be a simple, fun, and cheap way to connect with others.

First of all, let's vanquish those "shoulds" and "oughts" from our heads—they're not invited to our party! Fear has no place here; we're after shared time with people we care about or would like to get to know better.

Second, start simply—especially if you're new to hosting.

Instead of a sit-down dinner, invite a handful of friends over for drinks and appetizers, or for coffee and dessert. If you are specific in your invitation, they'll not expect dinner. Your hours underscore this; say 5 p.m. for drinks or 8 p.m. for dessert.

Eliminate the frenzy of housecleaning by (1) straightening only the rooms company will see (don't forget the bathroom), (2) serving outdoors if the weather's warm, or (3) using plenty of candles in a dim room (there's no need to dust or vacuum because no one can see the dirt—and your home will look very romantic!).

You can make yourself crazy coordinating a date that works for everyone. So unless it's a special couple you're having over, it's best to just set a time that works for you and factor in that some won't be able to make it. Be sure to ask guests to RSVP.

As you grow more confident at entertaining, extend an invitation for easy and inexpensive hamburger barbecues, pizza or spaghetti feeds, or late pancake breakfasts on the weekend.

Cut expensives by omitting liquor or asking people to bring their own beverages. Always have juice and soft drinks on hand for the increasing numbers of people who don't drink alcohol. You might also invite guests to bring their own meat for barbecuing.

Most fun of all is a potluck. You supply beverages and perhaps a main dish, and ask guests to bring a favorite food. You may wish to assign salads, desserts, or casseroles to vary the fare, but I've never had a party end up all desserts. And what fun if it did!

Once I invited friends to a take-out potluck. They had to bring food they could get to go. We wound up with donuts, pizza, chicken, hand-packed ice cream—and one hamburger from a guy who didn't understand he was supposed to bring enough to share.

Serving buffet-style, instead of a sit-down dinner, lends an informal air that relaxes both you and your guests. This works for potlucks, brunches, and even desserts. You may want to supply a few TV trays, or unclutter the coffee or end tables so people can set down drinks or plates.

Feel free to be creative: Have guests bring a favorite beer, coffee, or ice cream for a tasting party. The day taxes fall due, invite friends to drop in late for a Poor Party; serve cheese and crackers on paper plates and wine in tin cans or mugs. Throw a Fourth of July picnic in your backyard or at a local park with all-American menu of hotdogs, potato salad, chocolate cake, and watermelon.

Entertaining is fun. And it can be easier and less expensive than an evening out.

WELCOMING NEW NEIGHBORS

The moving van squats at the curb, spewing out your new neighbors' possessions. You consider your choices:

1. Preheat the oven and flour your elbows rolling out a batch of welcome cookies.
2. Watch from behind the curtains, jealous that their couch is nicer than yours.
3. Draw the blinds and dismiss the whole scene, just as you ignored the previous tenants.

Chances are you'll face one of these decisions soon, because the average U.S. resident moves at least eight times in a lifetime.

Yet 72 percent of Americans say they don't even know their next-door neighbors. Apparently the friendly '50s are history.

But you can help create the neighborly '90s with the following suggestions for getting to know that new person next door, across the street, or down the hall.

As for loving your neighbor? Well, that's up to you.

- Offer to help move things if you see them struggling.
- Have a pizza delivered to their home the day they move in. You supply the beverage.
- Offer to take a few photographs of them directing the movers or posing on their new porch.
- Take over a plate of cookies—store-bought megachip if you don't have time to bake.
- Provide them a new map of the city.
- Get informational brochures from the chamber of commerce, visitors' center, realty office, or apartment managers and put them in your neighbor's mailbox.
- Write down phone numbers of your doctor, dentist, day-care center or sitter, and hairdresser, and share them.
- Offer to share your newspaper until they start their subscription.
- Let them know about garbage and recycling pickups.
- Be host for an informal neighborhood get-together so they can meet people.

- Bring them fresh batteries for the smoke alarms.
- Assemble a little care basket with first-night goodies: soap, tooth-paste, toilet paper, perhaps instant coffee, rolls, and fruit for breakfast.
- Have your children show their children the school and park.
- Invite them to call on you if they have any questions, need help, or feel lonely.
- Mark on a map the locations of the closest grocery store, barber-shop, car wash, movie theater, library, etc.
- Take over a welcome treat for their pet, along with the business card of your favorite veterinarian.
- Invite them to let you know if your TV, music, kids, or dogs are ever too loud.
- Offer to baby-sit while they run errands.
- Be sensitive to their need for privacy; don't overwhelm them.

THE VALUE OF OLD FRIENDS

"That's what friends are for, that's what friends are for." The lyrics from the popular song hummed in my heart as I scrubbed the tub and dusted the house.

Pat was coming. For the first time in the twenty-six years I'd lived in Oregon, she was actually coming to visit me.

We met in Southern California when we were both nine years old. My dog clamped his teeth down on her ankle as she rode her bike past my house. Her leg healed and our friendship flourished.

I moved to Northern California at sixteen, and we visited and wrote regularly. She was my maid of honor, and I was her matron of honor, the one her mom asked to "tell Patsy the facts of life before her honeymoon."

Although we continued to send birthday cards, our lives went separate ways and the visits were few. Years later we suddenly had lots in common again.

Now here she was with her mother, bustling through suitcases in my bedroom and again putting on makeup using one bathroom mirror. Instinctively I kept my distance to avoid getting whapped across the face by her ponytail—long since given way to a soft, blonde-gray bob. We arched our lips as we had learned to do more than thirty-five years ago, giggling girls putting on lipstick.

Who were these middle-aged women staring back at us, women now older than our mothers were when they seemed so ancient?

The next weekend brought another déjà vu when I made my annual trip to Ashland, Oregon, to hole up in a bed-and-breakfast with my friend Stephanie.

We met at age twenty-seven at a feminism conference at the coast, and soon discovered we were both divorced and raising kids just blocks from each other.

She moved away, and our letters were like life-preservers tossed from one to the other.

We nursed each other through divorces and remarriages, love affairs and career moves, home ownership and ailing relatives. And somewhere along the line, we stopped whining about what men were doing to us and began taking responsibility for our lives.

These weekends with friends of thirty-eight and nineteen years formed bookends to the chronicles of my life. And the benefits of long-term relationships became clear:

- Old friends provide continuity to our lives. They love us through good times and bad.
- As we grow older and parents die or spouses fall to divorce, lifelong friends are the only ones who remember us as children or young people. They can see past graying hair and bald spots to the ponytails and crewcuts.
- Old friends offer us context, reference points, while current friends know only who we are today. When we worry aloud about our kids (of any age), old friends can remind us that we were once just as unwise—and we survived.
- Old friends can provide puzzle pieces of our past. They remember people, places, and circumstances that we've long forgotten.
- Lifelong pals, with their stories and memories, help prove to our kids or grandkids that we really were once their age.
- Old friends can help us see the progress we've made in life. In youth we dreamed of what we'd be; old friends are in the best position to cheer when we reach our goals.
- Lifelong pals help us process the stages of life as we intimately share our joys and fears and heartaches.

These precious weekends with Pat and then Stephanie were proffered pieces of the past and the promise of the future all at once.

Who are *you* long overdue with for a letter, a phone call, a visit? Could just be they're missing you, too.

REFRESHING A FRIEND

The weeks had been difficult for the young woman: hours spent preparing for admission to the school she wanted, serious illness of a relative.

And just when she and her husband had planned to get away for the weekend, a death in the family.

If anyone needed nurturing, it was she.

How could I help?

By providing her some solitude and comfort. So we arranged just that. I'd be out Sunday morning at church and brunch; why didn't she come over for a nice soak in my tub? (She has only a shower.)

She jumped at the offer.

I scrubbed the tub and attached an inflatable plastic bath pillow to its back; hung fresh, fluffy towels; and set out an array of bath oils and lotions surrounding a candle for her to light.

In the kitchen, I arranged a variety of herbal teas for her to choose from, along with a thermos to keep her selection warm.

In the bedroom, I changed the sheets, fluffed the pillows, turned back the down comforter, and switched on the bedside lamp. I fanned a stack of women's magazines out on the bed and put out a fresh nightie along with a plate of cookies and fruit. I raised the blinds so the view of the forest and the pond, ducks, and birds was unimpeded.

What fun it was, trying to make my home special for her! I wanted it to feel to her like bed-and-breakfast inns do to me: cosseting, with no demands, as nourishing as visiting Gramma's house for the weekend.

After church, I lingered over brunch to give her the time to savor the solitude. When I did get home, she was dozing in bed—soaked, rested, and ready for a visit.

She'd loved it! Discovering each little surprise delighted her, and my efforts gave her just the nurturing she needed. Out of her own digs, there was nothing that needed doing—nothing for her to do but relax and indulge herself.

We built a fire and made more tea. She set up her art supplies and was drawing a still life of my Southwestern decor (cow skull on an Indian blanket) when I left for a movie that evening.

It's a toss-up as to who got more from the experience. She got the mini-vacation she sorely needed; I experienced the joy of giving. And it didn't cost either of us a cent.

Which serves as a reminder of two things: (1) Few of us get the nurturing we long for, and (2) we may want to rethink our gift-giving. We plod through the malls in search of a thing the person probably doesn't even need. (Quick, what did you get for the birthday before last?)

Aren't there ways we can put the two together, giving experiences instead of objects? These unique gifts are likely to mean more, refresh both recipient and giver, be memorable, and may even cost less. Such a deal!

Let's look at some ways to share ourselves and what we have with friends and relatives:

- Provide a mini-vacation as described above. It's especially good for a friend who relishes the idea of getting away from a houseful of kids.

- Lend a beach or mountain cabin, a boat, or a motor home for a short vacation.

- Offer respite care for children or an ill person so the friend can get out for a walk, meal, movie, or visit with friends.

- Give a day's housecleaning, a carwash, yard cleanup.

- Cook a special meal and cater it in their own home. (Why wait for a funeral to do this?)

- "Kidnap" the person for a day of unexpected delights: a drive in the country, a picnic, brunch in a favorite restaurant.

- Indulge their passion: drive them to garage sales; treat them to a sporting event; go antiquing, hiking, visiting plant shops and nurseries.

- Proffer a book of coupons redeemable at any time: fresh-baked cookies, a carwash, a movie, lawn mowing.

- Cushion a "sick day" when a pal's under the weather physically or emotionally. Visit with chicken soup, a rented movie, a new magazine, a flower. Fluff up pillows, tell a joke, and skedaddle.

Giving—and getting—the precious gift of self nurtures our souls.

Starting a Social Support Group

In these time-strangled times, it helps to have connections—and times—you can count on.

I know four middle-aged women who are pals with a purpose. Alternating homes, they meet for dinner every Tuesday night. After a low-cal meal cooked by that's evening's hostess, they get to work.

They've organized Judy McCrery Drescher's bazillion books. Whipped Linda Zenicanin's patio into shape. Made decorations for Janet Moats's daughter's outdoor wedding. Hauled out bag after bag from pack rat Artha Gardner's home.

These friends do informally—and for free—what some people pay for: help with chores they don't seem able to complete on their own. They take up the slack left by families who live too far apart.

"We're more than friends—we're just like sisters," says Artha. "I didn't realize how lonely I was till I got into this group."

Originally begun for the purpose of losing weight and eating better, this group is now chow, chatter, and chores. All members of the same church, they have become dear friends who know they can count on one another any day of the week.

They've taken Linda to the hospital, organized Artha's recipes, cleaned out Judy's old office when she moved, and cheered one another when depressed. Plus, they play: they share games, reading out loud, car trips, birdwatching. "The four of us can count on each other completely," says Linda. "That's the biggest thing. I don't have family around—and they're more than family."

Susan and Jim Abrams also felt that need.

They'd gotten to talking about how life's fast pace allowed months to pass without their seeing close friends. Could they do something that didn't make life more complicated yet added quality?

They hit on the idea of dinner every Friday night with good pals Donna Roy and Joel Young. The women are cousins and grew up together in Maine; the men are native Oregonians and enjoy each other's company.

And to make the arrangement even easier, they worked out a plan: The couple cooking that Friday would have their weekly grocery shopping done by the other family. Every week, they switch.

"It makes life simpler and enriches life by having these other people a regular part of it," says Sue. "If we're off on vacation, we really miss them."

A typical Friday begins about 6 p.m., often with the four adults arriving at separate times. They'll have a glass of wine, eat, then chat. Occasionally, they'll take a walk or watch a video.

But conversation—especially about the value of community— engages this forty-something foursome most. The kids have fun, too.

Meals are simple—frequently pastas and ethnic fare. In eighteen months, they've missed perhaps a half-dozen meals because of illness, death in the family, or vacations.

Rarely, dinner is switched to Thursday if Fridays are impossible, but the show goes on if at least one person of each couple can make it.

"It's become a tradition," Donna acknowledges. "I think it's healthy for families to have traditions and to see that people can share things on a regular basis."

"It's given us some much deeper contact and connection with people outside our nuclear family," says Sue. "There's a richness now."

And that's what friends are for.

10. Conscious Kids

If our American way of life fails the child, it fails us all.
—Pearl Buck, *Children for Adoption*

Think back to childhood: Did you carry a datebook? Schedule time to play with friends? Wonder why you never had a free moment?

Of course not. But take a look at your kids' or grandkids' lives, and that's what you'll find.

Experts call today's kids hurried, rushed, pressured—even "pint-sized pressure-cookers." It's as if we're training kids to be the stressed-out, overachieving, no-time-for-that-now creatures we've become.

This problem has been getting attention from people who care about children, such as Richard Louv, author of *Childhood's Future*. They point out that we are too often:

Overstructuring kids' time. We may be so afraid of idle time ourselves (lest we be regarded as slackers or start facing uncomfortable feelings) that we're equally discomfitted seeing our kids do nothing. So we teach them to be workaholics, perpetual-motion machines who also will be unable to acknowledge, express, and appropriately act on their feelings.

Expecting perfection. We may gauge our own worth by what we accomplish, and we judge our children on the same false standards—which encourages our kids to feel they are loved based on what they do. (I'm OK if I get an A but not a D.) It also inculcates the old "I'll be OK or happy when . . ." syndrome: I'll be OK when I graduate from college, get married, have kids, when the kids get into school, when they leave home, when I get a raise/divorce/nose job.

Giving kids stuff instead of time. We feel guilty spending so little time with our children, so we throw money and activities and "opportunities" at them to absolve our guilt. When kids get stuff instead of attention, they also get the message that they're not really important to us, that money equals love, and that things mean happiness. We're setting them up to be voracious consumers and compulsive spenders for whom more will never be enough.

Giving more than we got and resenting it. We may wish our own parents were more attentive, so we go to all our kids' games, cart them to lessons, and give up the activities we'd like to do. Then we feel martyred and resentful about all the good we do for them. "You don't know how good you have it. Why, if I had half the opportunities when I was a kid that I give you . . . ." We may be sending children mixed signals and teaching them that parents deserve nothing and kids deserve all. Are we overcompensating?

Perhaps it's time to reassess the busyness of our children's lives and set some priorities:

- Spend time with them. Let's knock off the quality-time charade and stop putting them off. Frequent and undivided attention is the greatest gift we can give these precious little people. Just ask people whose children have grown—or died.

- Stop scheduling all their time. "Free time" allotted for something is not truly free time. Let's give them what we enjoyed: time to climb trees, see shapes in clouds, devour books, build forts. Playing spontaneously alone and with others engenders creativity, competence, cooperation, and problem-solving.

- Love our kids for *who* they are, not for what they accomplish. Kids shouldn't have to make us look good, hold our marriages together, or help us feel better about ourselves.

- Realize that our children do not belong to us. They belong to themselves—with their own dreams, talents, and interests. They come to us as buds, and it's our job as parents to nurture them toward full bloom.

Childhood goes by fast enough without hurrying our kids through it.

FOSTERING SPIRITUALITY

What comes to mind when children's spirituality comes up?

Guilt because you don't take your kids to religious services (or you do send them but stay home yourself)? Resentment over your own childhood religion? Embarrassment because you don't feel comfortable in a church or synagogue?

Many parents and grandparents fit into one of these categories. We work hard to give our children comfortable homes, good educations, nutritious meals, and lessons in everything.

But how well do we help our kids feel connected to the universe, confident that things will work out and that they will be essentially safe in this crazy, wonderful world?

We need improvement here or children miss something vital, says Jean Grasso Fitzpatrick, a New York theology student and founder of Generation to Generation, an ecumenical network for families' spiritual nurturing. She's the author of *Something More: Nurturing Your Child's Spiritual Growth*.

Let's note that we're discussing spirituality, not necessarily religion. (Think of the first as a generic connection to the Source, and the second as a brand-name connection.) Spirituality is housed in the heart rather than in a church or temple.

Fitzpatrick defines spirituality as an extended sense of home. Not only is the child related to parents and siblings but also to the neighborhood, city, country, and globe—"the underlying love in the universe that people call God."

This includes a sense of hope, gratitude, living in the present moment, and what she calls "seeing the miracle in everyday life."

Children are naturally spiritual, she contends. Just take a toddler for a walk around the block and see them exult in the slow-motion of a slug, the plink of rocks dropped through a grate. Witness the expression of a baby taking its first steps, a six-year-old venturing a wobbly ride sans training wheels.

Here is simple joy.

"We're so busy dragging them around to do the things we think are important that we miss those moments," Fitzpatrick says ruefully.

Spirituality isn't something we can stick on someone else; we have to feel it ourselves. We can't pay lip service to it and have it register on our children.

Whatever it is that we want to nurture in our children, "you have to make sure that Jesus or reincarnation or whatever means something to you in your heart—or it's a cheat to the child, because you're passing on something like Santa, just a name," Fitzpatrick says.

Here are some ways we can foster spirituality in our kids (and ourselves):

- Reconsider the religion of our childhood and see if we can't resume or adapt some of those teachings.
- Shop around for a place of worship in which we feel comfortable and inspired—and accompany our children there.
- Involve our kids in our community-service work to demonstrate the importance of caring about others.
- Spend time with our kids, giving them what they want most—our time and attention.
- Spend time in nature, looking and listening, without noisy, man-made distractions such as radios and recorders.
- Join with another family or two for periodic meals and celebrations to create a sense of community.
- Adapt religious rituals and traditions to fit our needs or create our own (blessings before meals, time for meditation, recounting of the day's happy events).
- Read and tell folktales from around the world to help children understand that people are the same all over.

The goal, Fitzpatrick says, is to help children see that "these are our people around us—not just our little family trying to end up on top of the heap."

KIDS NEED PARENTS WITH A LIFE

When does a good mother overdo it?

The question arose recently after separate visits with two mothers. I heard one ask her eleven-year-old if she'd gone to the bathroom. And the other gave such complicated instructions about prayers, tooth-brushing, and goodnight songs that no sitter could possibly have followed them.

And I heard about the mom who walked her ten-year-old, an only child, across the street to a friend's home for a sleepover, complete with color-coordinated new sleeping bag, radio, and alarm clock. She called to see how dinner went, then phoned again at bedtime.

My silent response to all of the above was: Get a life! Or maybe a job.

But the issue isn't mothers at home versus mothers who work. The issue is mothers in balance.

Being an effective mother and a happy woman calls for balance. No mother means to hurt her children, but sometimes that happens when she goes to the extreme of focusing too much attention on them. It's too easy to fall into the trap of letting children's accomplishments or problems define her own self-worth.

Striking that balance isn't easy. At least it wasn't for me.

I was at home when my two oldest were babies. I sewed them matching dresses, held neighborhood birthday parties for the dog, and savored each new stage of development. I was a good mother—but bored. I'll never forget standing over the toilet, dunking a dirty diaper, and wondering what was happening to my brain.

When my third came along, I was working two and a half days a week. That seemed ideal. I was home with my children most of the time, but I had sufficient mental stimulation.

When they were a little older, I worked full time. (It was mandatory because I'd divorced.) I loved my exciting newspaper career but felt guilty about before- and after-school day-care and missing many school events.

At one end there was boredom, and at the other extreme, there was guilt. So where's the balance? In the middle. But that doesn't mean every mother needs to work part-time to be effective or happy.

I know mothers at home full time who write, volunteer, further their talents at arts and crafts, read widely, share their garden produce with neighbors, participate in discussion groups, and stay connected with the outside world.

Some even put their children in day-care two days a week or bring in a sitter for a couple afternoons in order to have time to themselves. They recognize that children fill up our hearts but not always our heads.

How does a mother tell if she's smothering her child and neglecting herself? Make a pie chart on a piece of paper. How much time belongs to your children? Your husband? Your employer? Yourself? If one segment is just a sliver, you're probably out of balance.

And mothers face tremendous adjustment when their children leave home. With four grown sons gone, one woman realized she was clinging to her husband, which didn't work because she likes opera and he'd rather fish. She realized she couldn't depend on anybody else for her happiness—and she followed her youngest to college. More women should try it, she says.

Virginia Woolf wrote about the importance of women having a room of their own. Every mother needs one—even if it's just child-free space in her head.

LEARNING FROM OUR CHILDREN

Do you ever feel like a seesaw parent, swinging back and forth between extremes?

The kind of parents we become is imprinted on us by the kind of parenting we had as children: if our parents were quick to spank, chances are we will be, too.

Some of us vow that we will not be the controlling types our parents were—so we bend over backward to be a good guy and to give our children little discipline or limits.

Many of us see our mates as too harsh or too lenient, so we work to balance that out.

Sometimes we fight it out: "You coddle him—he'll never learn the rules!"

"You're too strict with her—she's got to grow up sometime!"

Sound familiar?

And where is the child as we parents replay or rebel against our own childhoods? Too often, their needs as developing human beings—and as little individuals—are overlooked as their parents battle over child-rearing philosophies.

To kids, it seems they are always at the "don't" end—don't do this, don't ever do that.

These suggestions from an unknown source reverse the list—and provide some balance—with these tips for parents:

21 Don'ts from Your Child

1. Don't spoil me. I know quite well that I ought not to have all I ask for—I'm only testing you.

2. Don't be afraid to be firm with me. I prefer it. It makes me feel more secure.

3. Don't let me form bad habits. I have to rely on you to detect them in the early stages.

4. Don't make me feel smaller than I am. It only makes me behave stupidly "big."

5. Don't correct me in front of other people if you can help it. I'll take much more notice if you talk quietly with me in private.

6. Don't make me feel that my mistakes are sins. It upsets my sense of values.

7. Don't protect me from consequences. I need to learn the painful sometimes.

8. Don't be too upset when I say, "I hate you." It isn't you I hate but your power to thwart me.

9. Don't take too much notice of my small ailments. Sometimes they get me the attention I need. Give me more attention at other times.

10. Don't nag. If you do, I shall have to protect myself by appearing aloof.
11. Don't make rash promises. Remember that I feel badly let down when promises are broken.
12. Don't forget that I cannot explain myself as well as I would like. That is why I'm not always very accurate.
13. Don't tax my honesty too much. I am easily frightened into telling lies.
14. Don't be inconsistent. That completely confuses me and makes me lose faith in you.
15. Don't put me off when I ask questions.
16. Don't tell me my fears are silly. They are terribly real, and you can do much to reassure me if you try to understand.
17. Don't ever suggest that you are perfect or infallible. It gives me too great a shock when I discover that you are neither.
18. Don't ever think that it is beneath your dignity to apologize to me. An honest apology makes me feel surprisingly warm toward you.
19. Don't forget that I love experimenting. I couldn't get on without it, so please put up with it.
20. Don't forget how quickly I am growing up. It must be very difficult for you to keep pace with me, but please do try.
21. Don't forget that I can't thrive without lots of understanding love.

Any parent who can heed these twenty-one rules for twenty-one years will have reared a happy, healthy child.

Easing Moving Traumas

Are you—or someone you know—the one in five Americans who'll move this year?

Moving can be traumatic. It's right up there with death and divorce, stress studies show.

Moving can be even harder on kids, because they don't have an adult perspective. They don't realize yet that one can keep old friends and make new ones as well.

For kids—especially teens—moving cross-country or even across town can seem like the end of the world. If parents emphasize moving as an adventure—emphasizing the unknown good about to unfold—it may help lessen the pain.

Right after my sophomore year in high school, my family moved from Southern to Northern California. I hated leaving my pals and the school newspaper. Little did I know that in my new town, I'd be president of the drama club, editor of the school paper, Miss Sonoma County—and meet the father of my three children.

So here's some help to make your move easier and help the kids adjust.

Involve the Kids

- Discuss the moving process with the kids; get them involved in what they want to keep, what to give away. Consider having them trade a favorite toy or stuffed animal with a best friend so they can take a part of their pal with them.

- Provide an address book so they can record friends' addresses, phone numbers, and good-bye messages.
- Give the kids an inexpensive camera and scrapbook so they can capture friends, school chums and teachers, the neighborhood, the house, and their room. The same can be done at the new house. (Have double copies made so they can share their new surroundings with friends back home.)
- Have the kids select a cache of postcards from the old and new towns so they can show new friends where they came from and share their new city with old friends.

PREVIEW THE NEW PLACE

- If the new location is nearby, take the children to visit their new home and school before the actual move.
- If the location is distant, have someone take and send photos of the new house, school, parks, or whatever might interest your child. Older children can write to the chamber of commerce or visitors' center of their new city for brochures on fun things to do.
- Have the kids draw the layout of their new room or come up with a decorating theme. Moving is a good time to replace bedspreads and curtains, so let the children choose.

REASSURE THE KIDS DURING THE MOVE

- Allow each child to pack a special suitcase or backpack of treasured belongings they can hand-carry to their new home.

- Assure the kids that children in their new neighborhood are aware that a new family is coming and are eager to meet them.
- Consider allowing teenagers to stay behind and live with a friend you trust. Finishing out the school year or having much of the summer with old friends can make the move less abrupt. Staying with a girlfriend's family for a few weeks made my high school move less traumatic.

SPEND TIME WITH THE KIDS UPON ARRIVAL

- Set up a younger child's room first. This is comforting to them.
- As soon as possible, tour your new town's interesting sights. Let the kids make a list for weekend trips: zoo, children's museum, park, trip to the beach or mountains, historical sites, and so on.
- If your child doesn't live with both parents, have them share photos of their new home, bedroom, yard, and school with the other parent. It's comforting for both child and absent parent to share their new surroundings.
- Allow a higher phone bill during the first two or three months after moving—especially for teenagers. The cost is worth the emotional comfort.
- Getting into school right away will help children of all ages make new friends, so consider moving in August.

CHILDREN LEARN BY IMITATION

To create conscious children, it helps to remember that children learn best by imitation. We can't say one thing and do another. This poem sums it up well:

IMITATION

If a child lives with criticism, he learns to condemn.

If a child lives with hostility, he learns to fight.

If a child lives with abuse, he learns to hurt others.

If a child lives with encouragement, he learns to be confident.

If a child lives with fairness, he learns to be just.

If a child lives with tolerance, he learns to be patient.

If a child lives with approval, he learns to like himself.

If a child lives with love, he learns to find love in the world.

—Anonymous

In her book, *The Sense of Wonder*, Rachel Carson makes a wise observation:

....

"If a child is to keep alive his inborn sense of wonder, he needs the companionship of at least one adult who can share it, rediscovering with him the joy, excitement and mystery of the world we live in."

What a privilege to be that person!

11. Angelic Altars

If you attend to the altar daily, you are symbolically attending to the sacred within yourself and in your world.
—Renee Beck and Sydney Barbara Metrick, *The Art of Ritual*

You may already have one and not even know it.

A table of treasured photos. A shelf of toys for your inner child. A windowsill holding a few prized items—a crystal, a shard of Anasazi pottery, a rock from the property you'd love to own.

They are personal altars. If that feels too churchy, call yours a sacred space or a contemplative corner.

More and more, people are creating special, beautiful sacred spaces to represent the things they are working on in their lives.

Some of us write about our issues in a journal. Others meditate, pray, or practice creative visualization. Some do what they call treasure-mapping. All are methods of clarifying what we're thinking, feeling, and needing. A personal altar does all these things in physical form.

The objects we choose for our sacred space represent something we want to manifest: compassion, appreciation for beauty, forgiveness, and so on. They merely are symbols of our intention to work on these issues—a lovely reminder that this is what we aspire to. The responsibility for change rests with us.

REASONS TO CREATE AN ALTAR

What should we create an altar for?

Celebrating who we are. Healing a childhood hurt. Working on a relationship (create an altar together, or separately). Letting someone go. Drawing peace to ourselves and the world. Healing illness. Nurturing ourselves through transition. Focusing our spiritual path (which is especially helpful if we're not involved with a church or temple).

Oralee Stiles, a spiritual healer in Portland, Oregon, creates altars for others. She made one for a friend undergoing brain surgery, another for her pregnant daughter. That altar contained a baby's shirt reading "Welcome to the world." After the birth, Stiles put it on her new granddaughter.

She's fashioned sacred spaces on bedside tables, windowsills, wall niches, shelves, mirrors, and in gardens. She's made temporary ones for friends atop restaurant tables and another on a coffee table for a memorial service.

Stiles enjoys personalizing a hotel room or guest room with a small altar when she travels. It makes you feel right at home, she says. (She starts by covering the TV with a pretty scarf.)

MATERIALS FOR AN ALTAR

These are some things you can use for your altar:

- Angels: figurines, paintings, dolls, drawings.
- Photographs: you at different stages, family members, friends, past loves, heroes.
- Natural objects: stones, crystals, seashells, leaves, nests, feathers, animal fur or bones.
- Toys: stuffed animals, old toys from your own childhood or your child's, alphabet blocks spelling out a name, dolls, magic wands, small puzzles, anything symbolic of a simpler or more innocent time.
- Living things: flowers, plants, fresh food.
- Beautiful objects: small paintings, candles, vases, prisms, old handiwork, stained glass, mirrors.
- Meaningful words: calligraphed sayings, prayers, affirmations, letters to yourself, letters from a loved one, significant quotations, fortunes from Chinese cookies, compliments others have paid you.
- Religious objects: rosaries, saints cards, figurines of Jesus or Buddha or St. Francis, goddesses, menorahs, crosses.

Suggestions for creating specific altars are detailed in *The Art of Ritual: A Guide to Creating and Performing Your Own Ceremonies for Growth and Change*, by Renee Beck and Sydney Barbara Metrick. I especially like their New Year's Eve altars, which can be set up around a room for a group to create meaning in their celebration.

To keep your altar effective, pay it attention—stay mindful of what you want to do. Flowers, plants, and fresh food force you to care for the altar, and lighting candles gets you involved. You can spend a few minutes each day with a sacred space, or whenever you feel the need.

What an altar is all about, of course, is spiritual love for others, for self, for the planet, for the creator.

In *Life's Companion: Journal Writing As a Spiritual Quest*, Christina Baldwin defines spiritual love as "a position of standing with one hand extended into the universe and one hand extended into the world, letting ourselves be a conduit for passing energy."

When you no longer see the altar (just as you grow oblivious to a picture that's been on the wall too long), it's time to update it to where you are now in your life—so you can continue passing energy.

What would your sacred space hold?

12. NATURE'S NURTURANCE

There is no word for "nature" in my language. Nature, in English, seems to refer to that which is separate from human beings. It is a distinction we don't recognize.
—Audrey Shenandoah, Onandaga Clan Mother, quoted in *Wisdomkeepers: Meetings with Native American Spiritual Elders*

Our society suffers from what I call "mall-aise." When we're bored or anxious or feeling a void deep within, we head for the mall.

What would suit us better is to head for the hills—and the lakes and the forests and the deserts and the rivers.

We've gotten so far removed from nature, from recognizing ourselves as a part of nature, that we're out of tune with the basic rhythm of the world.

We forget that humans—while spiritual beings—are fundamentally animals, as anyone who's given birth suddenly realizes. When we turn our backs on nature, we sever a section of our souls.

It's time to recognize what Native Americans have always known: Nature nurtures.

As Mathew King, Traditionalist spokesman of the Lakota people, points out in *Wisdomkeepers*: "It's time Indians tell the world what we know…about nature and about God.…You guys better listen. You got a lot to learn."

Or to put it in shopping-mall terms, Nature R Us.

Here are some ways to acknowledge that.

BRINGING NATURE INDOORS

Technology is wonderful, but high-tech can't replace the fundamental satisfactions of nature. We can incorporate the natural world into our homes by honoring the four elements: Water, Air, Fire, and Earth.

Here's how to bring the elements (or their representations) inside.

WATER

- Install a small waterfall or, easier yet, a portable, plug-in fountain in an entryway, living room, or bedroom—or on a deck or porch. Small fountains start at just over $100 and create a soothing splashing sound.
- Invest in a fishtank and discover the comfort of watching these colorful pets explore their watery world. Saltwater fish are more expensive than fresh.
- If you're in the market for a new home, buy or rent property adjacent to water: the sea, a lake, a stream, a golf-course water trap. Some apartment complexes boast man-made ponds and streams.

- Consider installing a waterfall, small stream, fishpond, or recirculating fountain outdoors, within view and earshot of the room where you spend the most time.
- Play audiotapes of the natural world: crashing waves, a tropical storm, splashing waterfalls, gurgling streams.
- Create a shallow reflecting pond on a porch or deck. Fill a wide, shallow, dark container with water to reflect clouds scudding overhead.
- Display reminders of water: seashells, driftwood, fishing lures, smooth river rocks.
- Hang posters, photographs, or paintings: seascapes, waterfalls, lakes.

AIR

- Hang wind chimes near a door or window.
- Open windows wide to let in the breeze.
- Add a screen door to the front or back door to ensure crosscurrents of fresh air.
- Hang light curtains during warm weather to stir in the breeze.
- Get a bird for a pet.
- Regularly hang pillows, comforters, and couch throws outdoor to air.
- Install a ceiling fan or display hand-held fans on the wall.
- In warm weather, sun-dry sheets and towels for that old-fashioned outdoor fragrance—and save on electricity or quarters for the dryer.

- Rearrange a couch, easy chair, or bed so that you can see trees ruffled by a breeze.

FIRE

- Use your fireplace often. Staring into a fire, listening to the crackle, is a fundamental pleasure instilled in us long ago.
- Don't reserve candles for birthdays and holidays. Use them to make any meal special. (We once enjoyed breakfast by candlelight on a gloomy morning.) Bathe by the warmth of candlelight. Scatter candles through the bedroom or living room for a romantic glow.
- If you don't have a fireplace, create the illusion of one by clustering all colors and sizes of candles on a foil-covered cookie sheet and placing it on a low table or the floor.
- Too warm for a fire in the hearth? Group candles in the fireplace.
- Hang crystals or prisms in windows or from lighting fixtures to refract and throw small rainbows around the room.
- Place candles in front of mirrors or windows to reflect their light.
- Display colored bottles (or plain ones filled with colored water) on a sunny windowsill.
- Create your own ceiling galaxy with stick-on, glow-in-the-dark stars and planets.
- Adopt New Mexico's holiday custom of luminarias (also called farolitos) to outline paths, fence tops, and even roof lines. Simply roll down the top of a lunch-size brown bag, weight it with sand, and place a votive candle inside. The warm glow

lights the way for visitors. Electric luminarias are also available in Southwest catalogs.

EARTH

- In sunny climes, surround yourself with Mother Earth by building with adobe. Or create the effect by texturing walls to resemble this mixture of earth and water. (See "Have Fun with Color" in Chapter 3, "Restful Rooms.")
- Display crystals, polished agates, cut geodes, and other lovely minerals—God's gift from the ground.
- Surround yourself with houseplants nestled in terra-cotta pots.
- Build with and leave exposed natural materials such as wood, stone, and brick. Use grasscloth and cork wallcoverings.
- Decorate with bird nests, tree limbs, fruit, leaves, dried flowers, pinecones, and grapevine wreaths and swags.
- In furniture and accents, choose logs, twigs, and wicker.
- Use carvings and pictures of flowers, birds, fish, and animals.
- Let the seasons dictate decor by using centerpieces and accents of whatever's in season: pumpkins, squash, Indian corn, and nuts in fall; bare branches and pinecones in winter; forced bulbs and early-blooming plants in spring; fresh fruit, flowers, and feathers in summer.
- Bring the outdoors in with decorating aids such as watering cans, birdhouses, old skiis and snowshoes, fishing creels and poles, and so on.

Grow Your Soul by Gardening

Every dedicated gardener knows the therapeutic joys of digging in the dirt, cajoling plants skyward, harvesting the fruits of their labors after working with—and despite—the elements.

Those of us with the space or inclination can landscape, cultivate flowers, plant a vegetable garden. But those of us with limitations, such as condo, apartment, or houseboat dwellers—or people who are physically limited—can also become gardeners of our souls.

We can cultivate on a smaller scale:

Houseplants

Develop a green thumb by starting with easily grown plants such as philodendron, ivy, bromeliad, spider plant, wandering Jew, sansevieria, prayer plant, ficus, or peperomia. Buy a houseplant book and ask questions at your local garden shop. This hobby can become addictive.

Window Gardens

On windowsills inside or in window boxes outside, we can nurture herbs for our kitchens, cuttings from friends' yards, and flowers such as geranium, nasturtium, and petunia for small but lush gardens.

Container Gardens

On decks, porches, and fire escapes, we can create a veritable jungle with the proper containers and know-how. Even veggies—tomatoes, lettuce, and peppers—can flourish. Again, ask questions and don't be afraid to learn by trial and error. Bottle gardens indoors are also fun—

and when hermetically sealed, don't require watering. (It's the ideal garden for travelers!)

Bonsai

The term means "a plant in a pot." Bonsai began in China in 300 B.C. and moved to Japan in 1200 A.D. These tiny trees (or shrubs or herbaceous plants) may be grown indoors or out from seeds and cuttings from beech, elm, oak, maple, pine, juniper, lilac, yew, and others. A different Japanese name exits for each type of these trained plants: landscapes, windswept, top growth, root over a rock, cascade, and more. A fine hobby for the disciplined and patient!

Attracting God's Creatures

Here's how to welcome birds, butterflies, and small animals to your yard:

- Leave or restore a part of the yard to its natural state of indigenous growth.

- Plant fruit and seed-bearing trees and bushes which provide food and shelter—cherries, apples, crabapples, hawthorns, and blueberry bushes. Some are messy, so don't plant them near streets, walks, or patios. Hummingbirds are drawn to honeysuckle, silk trees, and orange-red trumpet vines.

- Attract butterflies to an area with direct sun for at least six hours a day. Plant butterfly bush, cosmos, zinnia, nasturtium, black-eyed Susan, verbena, and bee balm. You may want to add a butterfly-hibernation box on a well-sheltered pole or tree.

- Leave dry dog food out for raccoons, but not regularly or they will come to depend on you, which isn't healthy for wild animals.
- Decide which you value more: cats or birds. If it's a toss-up, confine kitty to the house so birds feel safe in your yard.

BIRD FEEDERS

Feeders come in all sizes and shapes and are generally inexpensive. They're naturals for bird-watchers or for anyone who wants to learn more about our feathered friends. The birds will light long enough for you to be able to look them up in your bird-identification book. Feeding birds will provide hours of delight for anyone, including shut-ins and children.

Select a feeder which protects the seed (and maybe the birds) from rain, or the seeds will mold or even sprout. Clean the feeder regularly and keep it filled. Sunflower seeds will attract the greatest variety of birds. If you buy a new feeder, put it near the old one so the birds can find it. Bug-attracting plants near feeders will help attract insect-eating birds.

The grandkids and I fashioned our own bird treats by slathering pinecones with a mixture of peanut butter and birdseed, then fastening them to my deck railing. I think the kids enjoyed it more than the birds!

BIRDBATHS

A bird in the hand may be worth two in the bush. But three in the birdbath are even more delightful. That's why birdbaths are popping up in yards like mushrooms after a spring rain. They're decorative, they attract a variety of birds, and their prices—from free to nearly $500—correspond to anyone's means. Look for birdbaths at garden shops or bird specialty stores

Birds bathe two to three times daily if they get the chance, in either water or dust, to control insects on their plumage, according to the Audubon Society.

Birdbaths will attract to your yard birds that don't use feeders, such as warblers, orioles, and tanagers. Birdbaths come in assorted types: traditional, modern, mounted, and recirculating. Or make your own cheaply. Hang a bucket from a tree; perch an upside-down garbage-can lid on an inverted tile drainpipe weighted with rocks; put a ceramic saucer on a chiseled stump or log; use a basin set in the ground; or use a naturally hollowed river rock. Big plastic plant saucers are handy and cost just $5 for one twenty inches across.

A hose nozzle set on mist and hung over a branch will also attract birds, as will a soaker hose emitting mist or fine spray and turned on at regular times.

PETS AS HEALERS

One of the best ways to stay in tune with nature—aside from having a baby!—is caring for a pet. Some researchers say our natural bond with animals is primeval, harkening back to early humans' respect for the power of an animal's spirit.

Today, society has rediscovered that healing power, using animals not only as eyes and ears but as "seeing hearts." Medical studies show the value of pets:

- Pet owners have lower cholesterol and blood pressure; so pets may prevent heart disease.
- Older persons who have a pet see a doctor less frequently than seniors who don't keep animals.
- Therapists are sucessfully using animals with mentally and emotionally disturbed children and adults.
- Aquariums in medical offices soothe anxious patients; dental patients are less nervous before surgery.
- Pet owners in general report fewer health problems and say they are happier than people without pets.

Pets offer what we all long for: unconditional love. They provide us the opportunity to care for something beside ourselves, to reach out. Perhaps that's why 60 percent of Americans keep pets.

To be loved, we must love. Is there a void in your life a pet might fill?

CREATING A VIEW

Living in a suburb at the bottom of a hill in a wooded ravine, I'm fortunate to gaze out on trees and a pond complete with ducks and even a beaver dam. Watching the changing seasons up close gives me great joy and serenity.

But even without this, we can create a window on the natural world:

- Plant potted trees, shrubs, and flowers on a porch, deck, or fire escape.

- Fill window boxes with flowers for a flash of color and an air of European charm.
- Hang a wallpaper mural of a mountain, lake, ocean, desert, or sylvan scene.
- Build a trellis or latticework outside a window which looks onto a parking lot or into a neighbor's window. Hang plants from the lattice, or train vines up over it for beauty and privacy.
- Hang a stained-glass window of a natural scene in a viewless window and enjoy the play of sunlight through the colors.
- Double an attractive view by placing a large mirror or mirror tiles (or mirrored closet doors) on the wall opposite.
- Display posters, paintings, or large photographs of outdoor scenes.
- Block an unpleasing view by hanging plants or by placing them on an elevated plant stand in front of the window.
- Create a picture window by mounting an old window frame on the wall over a poster of the outdoors. You may want to add shutters on the sides to complete the window effect, or add a shelf or window box to the bottom of the frame.
- Hire an artist to paint a natural scene on a wall.

SAVORING THE SEASONS

If time seems to be slipping away ever more quickly, it's definitely time to savor the small miracles of each month.

It was midsummer already, but the delicious season seemed to be passing me by. Sure, I'd been on a cruise and entertained relatives, but somehow it seemed that summer hadn't registered yet.

It occurred to me that the secret to savoring the seasons—which seem shorter the older we get—is to define what we enjoy most about each of them, then take the time to get it, do it, feel it, and see it. After I made a summer list and experienced some of those joys, I no longer felt angry at August.

Here's what I came up with for each season.

SPRING

Transforming my bedroom decor. Washing windows and deciding that they must have built the smudges into the glass at the factory. Braking for the first garage sales of the season. Decorating an Easter tree with the grandkids by hanging eggs and signs of spring on an attractive bare branch stuck in a vase. Planting flowers and herbs in pots on the deck. Staging a scavenger Easter-egg hunt with hollow plastic eggs and printed instructions on the inside as to where to find small gifts. Eating asparagus.

SUMMER

Going barefoot. Lounging all day at the lake. Making salads instead of cooking. Drinking pink lemonade with a sprig of mint. Picking berries. Going to the county or state fair and enjoying everything from food to critters to hobby collections to funny-shaped squashes to rapid-fire-delivery demonstrations of those slicer/dicer gizmos. Arranging summer flowers in an old pitcher. Falling asleep in the sun. Lazing in a hammock. Barbecuing chicken and hamburgers. Taking a car trip. Splashing in a downtown fountain. Eating watermelon and cherries and seeing how far I can spit the seeds. Cooling off on a hot day at a movie matinee. Reading a novel. Eating outdoors. Driving through the country in late August to inhale the freshly cut hayfields.

FALL

Scavenging windfall apples and making applesauce and apple crunch. Going to Oktoberfest celebrations. Making a Halloween tree with the grandkids. Gathering oats, wheat, weeds, and cattails alongside the roadside for making dried arrangements. Buying school supplies with the grandkids. Inviting women friends over for a Sunday afternoon potluck. Tramping through the woods to savor the changing colors. Picking out pumpkins in the country.

WINTER

Watching snow fall. Sleeping on flannel sheets under a down comforter. Taking a rain walk without an umbrella and getting soaking wet. Wearing bulky sweaters. Darting from antique store to antique store in the rain. Wearing teal-colored rainboots and walking in the puddles. Holing up in a cozy beach cabin and watching a storm. Making breakfast for dinner and getting in bed to eat it, with a stack of magazines for dessert. Feeding the birds and watching them. Making big pots of stew or chili and having family or friends in to help eat it. Losing track of time in a bookstore. Turning on music and staring at the fire.

Maybe next year you could spend a week's vacation doing just these simple things instead of traipsing off to see the world.

What do you love about each season? Are you giving it to yourself?

TREES AS LIVING LEGACIES

Ever wonder about what to give the person who has everything, the newborn or the senior who doesn't need another knickknack?

Plant a tree in their honor!

This can be done in a number of ways: Give them a seedling or balled tree to plant as they please. Send money in their name for a planting in Israel or in a local reforestation project. Donate a tree in their name to a park, school, or low-income housing project. Or plant one in your yard.

At age thirteen, I planted trees at my junior high school with other student-body officers on Arbor Day. Thirty years later, the school is now a community center—but the saplings have soared, providing shade to people born after that planting.

One Mother's Day, I planted two rhododendrons in the common yard of our condominium complex in honor of my late mother and my husband's mom. For the years we lived there, we enjoyed watching them grow and bloom. Now others have that privilege. I've since installed a lilac bush—Mom's favorite—outside the bedroom window in my new condo.

A friend who lost a son planted an evergreen in a nearby arboretum. She feels close to him each Christmas when she goes there to decorate "his tree."

Children of any age enjoy watching "their" trees grow. Even when they're adults and you've moved away, they delight in driving past the old house pointing out their trees to their children: "That's the maple we planted when I turned ten!"

Trees are a practical, thoughtful, and lasting gift or memorial which honors both a person and Mother Earth. Consider them for birthdays, graduations, weddings, new-baby gifts, housewarmings. Use a loved one's ashes to nurture their special tree.

It feels good to be a modern Johnny Appleseed!

LESSONS IN A JAPANESE GARDEN

If your town boasts a Japanese garden, you've got grace in your own backyard. The lovely garden in Portland, Oregon, is just minutes from my home, the perfect retreat when I need a shot of serenity.

Here is peace and simplicity. At every turn among the flowering plums and cherries, the mossy stones and placid pools, is an invitation to look inward. Surrounded with symbolism, here is private space to take our emotional and spiritual pulse.

At the lower- and upper-level entries, imposing gates with tile-topped walls hide possibilities within; beyond lies the unknown. *What doors do I fear walking through?* Closing doors on different chapters of our lives can feel sad and frightening, but it puts us on another side with fresh views and exciting new options.

Those options include several paths we can take upon entering the garden. *How many times have I been paralyzed with indecision, fearful of choosing the wrong path?* The garden of life offers many paths, but we all reach the same destination sooner or later. Aside from crucial moral choices, perhaps the question isn't which path is best, but which path beckons me most right now? Few decisions are irreversible, and it's always possible to retrace our steps.

One of the beauties of a Japanese garden is that varied viewpoints are built in. Every overlook, every resting place provides a fresh way of seeing. *Do I realize that there's more than one way of seeing situations in my life?* To never consider other possibilities is to shut ourselves off from discovering new ways that may work better or offer more satisfaction.

A smaller path of leveled stones beckons down to the water for a closer view of the multicolored koi glimmering below the pond's surface. Various colors, assorted patterns, each unique. *Do I appreciate the differences of the people in my world?* It's amazing how much energy we expend trying to get people to be more like we are. Could we stand it if we succeeded? Perhaps it's time to enjoy those differences.

Here in the tea garden, two small shelters stand separate from the house. *Is there a place in or near my home where I escape life's clatter and hear the sounds of nature and my own private voice?* We all need, if not a room, at least a nook of our own away from the TV and the noise of family. A special place—or even the bedroom staked out for an hour—says: This is where I make time for me. I'm worth it.

Japanese footpaths are deliciously circuitous, an invitation to play. Remember the vacant lots of early childhood when we were too small to see over the weeds to where the path comes out? We simply had faith it would come out somewhere. *Am I reluctant to take detours, to explore a different way to my destination, to not always know the outcome?* We can break our routines by driving a different way home from work, trying a new restaurant, planning a vacation somewhere different. A path needn't become a rut.

In this part of the garden, stone paths wind past pools and water-falls. But in its movement, even water pauses to pool, to rest, to gather strength for the next eddy, the next tumble over rocks. *Do I pause to savor where I've been before rushing on to the next experience?* When we're always in motion, we have no time to reflect, to enjoy, to be here now.

In the sand-and-stone garden, seven rocks and a stone pillar stand starkly simple, surrounded by carefully raked gravel. *How simple is my life?* Is it so cluttered with things that I no longer see the few treasures I enjoy? So choked with acquaintances and activities I don't have time for the people and pleasures I love? This garden illustrates that less is, indeed, more.

A bamboo chute spills water into a stone basin, a tiny sound among the rushing waterfalls. *Do I stop to hear the small voice—the unspoken need of a friend, the plea of a child, my inner self struggling to be heard?* Listening only to the noise, we can miss the sound.

All this loveliness—and some lessons, too. (See Resources for cities which have Japanese gardens you can visit.)

TAKE TIME FOR A PICNIC

If we don't pack a picnic sometime between June and September, we haven't fully experienced summer.

A picnic is magical time-out from the frantic pace of everyday life. It's time to slow down, get back to basics.

Which is why some people hate picnics. (They often marry us folks who love them.) They ask pesky questions: "Why carry all this stuff so far when you can eat comfortably at home? Why sit on the ground and be miserable? Why mess with the ants and flies and bugs?"

"Because—just because," you stammer back.

Maybe picnics are wonderful because they get us away from the TV and into nature. Because they evoke something primitive in us. "Is the rock hot enough to cook on yet?" Because they reintroduce us to seeing the world up close: blades of grass, scavenging birds, pretty pebbles underfoot. Because they enforce leisure time with people we care about.

Picnics can be as simple or as fancy as you please. Fried chicken, potato salad, and watermelon are old-fashioned fun. Potlucks are great for a crowd. Hamburgers are perfect. Gourmet meals from a deli are romantic and hassle-free. But fast food can suffice, too.

A picnic can be great multigenerational family fun. A perfect lovers' tryst. A way to sit in the silence with yourself.

Picnics enable people of all ages to run off excess energy. Play games. Catch up on reading (preferably something meaningless and fun). Talk to each other. Go barefoot. Be silly. Snooze. Swim and dry off and get back into the water again.

But most of all, picnics are special. They make memories the way fast food on the fly simply doesn't.

As informal as picnics are, there are a few courtesies:

- Keep your dog on a leash. Not everyone enjoys a wet nose in their lunch.
- If the music of the waves or the lapping lake or the wind in the trees isn't enough for you, at least have the courtesy to bring earphones. Not everyone enjoys your kind of music.

- Don't bring work from the office. The people with you need your time and attention.
- Anyone who even thinks of bringing a cellular phone along on a picnic should be beaten about the ears with it by Smokey the Bear.

Now, where'd I put that plaid picnic blanket we've used for years?

LEARNING MORE ABOUT NATURE

One important way to draw closer to nature is to learn more about it. There are excellent books and educational films about everything from astronomy to wildflower identification.

Here are some suggestions:

- Take a class at the local Audubon Society. This is how I learned more about the beavers in my backyard.
- Obtain a simple guide to trees, birds, and flowers; keep it handy near a view window. How many species can you identify from your living room?
- Invest in a pair of binoculars.
- If natural science feels intimidating, start with children's books to easily understand geology, astronomy, oceanography, anatomy, and so on.
- Watch the TV listings for interesting programs on public broadcasting and the Discovery channel.
- Rent documentaries about the natural world from the library.

- Share books about nature with children. Not only will it educate you both, but it will help instill an appreciation and wonder for the gifts all around us.

When we take the time to feel our pulses pound, we remember that we are as much a part of nature as the wind and the sea.

13. CREATIVE CONSCIOUSNESS

Our creative dreams and yearnings come from a divine source. As we move toward our dreams, we move toward our divinity.
—Julia Cameron, *The Artist's Way*

Creativity is the natural life force working through us. The act of being creative is celebrating life.

If we're bored or complacent, it's time to expand our horizons or even rediscover an old pleasure. We can add zest to life by finding a passion—and this doesn't mean an obsessive relationship.

When we're passionate about a cause, a hobby, or even a vocation, we feel fully alive, we lose track of the time, we feel at one with the object of our passion and even with the universe.

How can we distinguish passion from compulsion? A passion enhances life for ourselves or others (at least it does no harm); a compulsion gets in the way of living fully. We can jump-start our creativity by making a list of things we love doing.

But many of us—particularly women—feel we're not creative. We tend to view creativity as being a famous artist or a well-known writer.

All of us, on a daily basis, are creative: The act of stretching a dollar is creative. Solving a tricky problem is creative. Planting a garden is creative.

Many of us long to become more creative. The stress of our lives impedes our creativity. Yet the very act of being creative—feeling a passion for something—is also an antidote to stress and even depression.

As we come to know who we are, we free our creativity to blossom. And as our creative force unfurls, we become more of who we truly are.

THE MANY PATHS TO SELF-DISCOVERY

No matter what your age, it's embarrassing and even frightening to admit that you don't really know who you are or what you want.

This realization can be activated at crucial life changes: divorce, addiction recovery, retirement, children leaving home, widowhood—even scaling down to a simpler lifestyle.

Each can leave you with empty hours, prompting the question: Who am I?

Years of focusing on other people or on work may have caused you to put your own needs, desires, and dreams on the back burner.

Alone, the heat is on; the time is now.

Here are some simple ways to begin to discover the unique, interesting person you are. Most of the techniques are used by various therapists.

Finish the Sentence

Without thinking it to death, complete these sentences: I've always wanted to . . . (run my own business, play piano, etc.). I wish I were more . . . (outgoing, studious, healthy, etc.). Finish these: I'd really like to . . . . When I'm gone, I hope people remember me for . . . . If I had just six months to live, I'd . . . . I'd like to try . . . . My idea of a perfect day is . . . . It's really important to me to . . . . I would . . . if I wasn't so . . . .

Set Up a "Self Shelf"

Clear a bookshelf; reserve it for material that interests you. Items might include books, magazine articles, newspaper clippings, travel folders, classified ads, job descriptions, hobby information, music, inspirational literature, or pictures. As the shelf fills up, you'll develop a picture of what you're about. Go ahead, be "shelfish."

Make Three Wishes

Wishing is the first step toward having; as your self-knowledge and self-confidence increase, you may become your own genie. Make a magic three wishes in these areas of your life: personal, work, family, dwelling, finances, and health.

Analyze Your Dreams

Psychologists say dreams are messages from the subconscious, that you can learn eight times faster what's really going on inside by dream analysis rather than by intellectual rehashing. To learn more, read books about dream interpretation and keep a dream journal, noting dream plots, characters, and how you felt. With practice, you'll decipher your own dream code.

Try Something New

Once a week, try something you've never done or haven't done for ages. Go to a square dance, a foreign movie, an ethnic restaurant. Read a book or article on something you know nothing about. Take a new route home. Strike up a conversation with a stranger. Attend a religious service, a concert, a lecture, a support group.

Fantasize

Make time to daydream; let your imagination run wild. Get started by filling in some more blanks: If money were no problem, I would.... A trip of a lifetime would be .... It would be wonderful if the family could .... The greatest job in the world would be ....

Trust Your Feelings

Start with the basics: Select the menu item that first strikes your fancy. If you get the urge to take a bubble bath, do it—don't argue that it makes no sense because tomorrow is your hair-washing day. Honor your impulse; don't talk yourself out of it.

Make Some Lists

Discover what's important to you by keeping running lists with titles such as: Things I Love. My Perfect Room (or House). What I Want in a Relationship. What I Like About Me. Compliments I've Received. Things I Want to Do. My Fears.

Keep a Journal

Whether it's a spiral notepad or a covered blank book, your journal becomes a private chronicle of growth as you reveal your secrets, fears, accomplishments, and dreams daily. If you need help getting started, read one of the books on journal-keeping.

Let's Stop Sabotaging Creativity

How do we know when we're being creative?

Many women liken it to pregnancy. You know you're doing something special, yet the process is bigger than you; you're on automatic. So it is when we lose track of time, giving ourselves over to the thrall of creative activity.

As wonderful as being creative feels, we often sabotage it.

Women, especially, do it with *perfectionism* ("I might not get it right"), *listening to our critical voices* ("Just who do you think you are?"), and *heeding the negative people around us* ("It'll never work").

Diane Ealy, author of *The Woman's Book of Creativity*, found that most studies about creativity are based on male models.

Women's brains work differently, she notes. Men tend to think in a linear fashion (which is often called "logical thinking"), while women create in a spiral mode that's very in touch with their feelings (which we can be shamed into believing is wrong).

When we stifle our creativity, we feel anger and even depression. Anger, Ealy says, is a good indicator we're off our own track.

We also experience burnout, she notes, when "we're going in the wrong direction, trying to be something we're not. When we try to pull ourselves away from creativity and the way we get nurtured, we drain our own energy and get exhausted."

That's evident when it's murder getting out of bed to go to a job we hate but easy to spring up on a Saturday morning to do something we love.

"Expressing ourselves creatively requires us to assume risks, make mistakes, experiment with the unknown, and take leaps of faith." Ealy points out. "These activities occur only when we're energized by a spirit of adventure and curiosity."

We foster our creativity when we're in touch with nature. Able to act spontaneously. Grant ourselves solitude. Develop a sense of humor. Follow our passion. Listen to our dreams. Heed our inner voice. Make our own space.

How can we nurture creativity in our kids?

"Leave them alone," Ealy advises. "Let them explore. Resist the temptation to 'fix' what they do or say, "That's not the way it's done.'"

Kids are naturally creative—until we stifle them.

As adults who care about kids, we can encourage their innate creativity by observing their interests.

Since he was tiny, my grandson Zach has demonstrated an interest in sports, so he plays Little League and takes karate lessons. He'd just scored high in science, so we bought him a children's science encyclopedia. Brittany is highly dramatic and gravitates toward the arts, so my art box is high on her list, and I recently took her to a children's theater production of *The Miracle Worker*. Ashley is musical and crazy for animals, so her mother got her a kitten. I take her to the zoo and a friend's farm, and we play different types of music when she visits.

As Ealy points out, when we validate creativity—in ourselves or our kids—it spreads enthusiasm and energy to all areas of our lives.

Creativity is contagious!

Harkening Back to the Child Within

We're all carrying around a little person who knows who we truly are, who knows what we really want, who remembers the secret of creativity.

For women, that little person is particularly important.

Emily Hancock, a Berkeley, California, therapist who teaches psychology at the Center for Psychological Studies, sees several reasons grown women feel unacquainted with themselves:

- Our culture encourages us to define ourselves by our relationships. Ask a man about when something happened, and he's likely to say, "Well, I was selling computers then." But a woman is more likely to say, "I'd just divorced Bill, so it must have been 1984."

- Men define maturity as striking out on their own; women have traditionally defined it by marrying.

- Working hard to prove ourselves professionally, women adopt male standards of success and lose sight of what's really important to us. What mother hasn't agonized over missing a child's first steps because we had to work?

"To achieve, women have had to forfeit their womanly concerns, strip down to their competence and outfit themselves in corporate drag," says Hancock.

Women juggling jobs and family grow accustomed to putting ourselves last. We're trying to deliver for our boss; we're trying to meet the kids' needs; and/or we're trying to placate a husband.

Where is the time—or energy—for us?

"Women need to retrieve their own purposes instead of simply harnessing their skills to the agendas of others," Hancock says.

"I don't recommend that women cross off their relationships, but I do recommend that women put themselves back into the picture and reclaim their own purposes."

But how?

In her book, *The Girl Within: Recapture the Childhood Self, the Key to Female Identity*, Hancock offers some solutions to the "Who am I?" dilemma.

To find out who you truly are, look back at who you were, she suggests. Recall who you were at age ten, for instance—before you began dressing to please others or curtailing your own interests in favor of some boy's.

The "girl within," says Hancock, "is the girl who pulls on her blue jeans, packs her lunch, and gets on her bike and goes to her best friend's house to build a treehouse.

"She's the girl who has a soaring sense of imagination and a boundless sense of competence. She wakes up in the morning and knows what she wants to do that day; she puts on clothes that please her. She's not doing anything that is somebody else's vision of her."

What fascinated you at ten? I loved to read—books on extrasensory perception and human quirks, on Abraham Lincoln and volcanoes. I led my younger sisters and friends on adventures, trekking down paths just to see where they came out. I scrambled over the foothills near our home—even though they were forbidden—and dreamed of one day seeing the world beyond the mountains.

Despite relationship entanglements and child-rearing, some of my greatest joys as an adult have been researching and writing stories about what makes people tick, visiting the Lincoln Memorial and reliving Lincoln's final hours in Washington, D.C., hiking through the world's largest volcanic crater, taking my kids on a two-month adventure through Mexico, and seeing much of the world.

And I still can't resist a path.

Sometimes, Hancock says, we have to get angry before we can break free. We have to get mad at whoever is creating the expectations that keep us from being who we really are. That anger, she says, "separates us from being subservient to the other's idea of who we are."

But love works, too—equal partnerships where women don't have to compromise the self.

"Women have been searching 'out there' for the answers," Hancock says. "They've overlooked the inner resources they have—this girl, this touchstone for their real identity."

How can the girl (or boy) *you* once were help you to be happier today?

We have only so much time and energy. So how do we spend it?

Too often, women are split between the things we love to do and the things we need to do.

We love singing, but we drop lessons to raise a family. We long to catch our child's school program, but an important meeting keeps us office-bound.

So often, life seems either/or: Women can prize relationships—or forgo having an intimate partner and focus on our careers. Many of us try to do both, yet constantly feel guilty about work or family.

And, too often, we feel cut off from ourselves. That disconnection from ourselves—that feeling we're living someone else's life instead of our own—doesn't have to happen. We don't have to be smiling for the world when we long to be singing from our own passion.

That's the message of Claudia Bepko and Jo-Ann Krestan in *Singing at the Top of Our Lungs: Women, Love, and Creativity.*

The family therapists specializing in gender issues and addiction contend that many women get addicted to booze, pills, shopping, or whatever because we are so split off from who we really are.

They urge women to examine what we truly love, just how we are most creative. By love, the authors mean that which touches our hearts; by creativity, they mean not artistic expression but what arouses our passion (playing the piano, rearing children, growing vegetables, being a CEO).

When we aren't living our passion, we don't feel alive. We may experience depression, anxiety, addiction, eating disorders, or that feeling that there's never enough time for ourselves.

To help determine just what type of creative being we are, Bepko and Krestan offer these four types (devised from responses to a survey):

Lover. Relationships are most important to her. She puts her energy into marriage, children, friendships. She often chooses crafts (projects which can easily be interrupted).

Artist. Her work comes first. People call her selfish, because women aren't expected to do this. Her energy is tremendously focused.

Leader. Her energy is primarily relational, and her concern for human connections takes a public form (often in health or service professions). These people are the most pressed for time.

Innovator. Her creativity is in the foreground and relationships in the background. She struggles more for a balance than the artist does.

After deciding what type we are, we can find the form that fits us— the lifestyle that fits our energies.

"Knowing what your form takes is critical to your well-being," says Krestan.

If relationships are more important to us than anything, we'd be miserable living across the country, cut off from family and friends—even if we are making big bucks. If running our own business is what makes us feel most alive, it will probably be a mistake to take on raising our husband's three kids by his first marriage.

Do you have a space of your own at home? That's one question Krestan asks women in order to determine if we're honoring our passions. Men usually do have a spot (workshop, garage, den, special chair), she finds. Too often, women don't.

That's why she advocates separate spaces for couples. It may be a woman's workroom, greenhouse, even her own bedroom. To honor our creative expression, we need not only space but time: "Women need to value their own time—not to use it more efficiently, but to value it more sufficiently," says Krestan.

We also need to value the creative process, not the product. It doesn't matter if the product of our creativity has no social usefulness; it matters only that we are excited, soothed, or stimulated by our passion—one sign being that we lose track of time while doing it.

Men can help women express their creativity by "getting out of their way" and not making competing demands, Krestan says. And men and women can help daughters find their own passionate voices by being good role models for them.

If you have a dream, she advises, begin today.

"Women who want to be alone aren't strange—they have the good taste to value their own company," Krestan says.

"Do the thing that you want most to do, first. And fit your responsibilities in around it."

PASSION: ANTIDOTE TO DEPRESSION

Sometimes creativity seems out of the question. For one thing, we're too darned bored. Even depressed.

Being blue doesn't mean there's anything wrong with us, says Seattle cultural anthropologist Jennifer James: "The only issue is to take care of yourself and do what you can to feel good again."

And that means finding our passion—valuing ourselves independently of any other relationships, particularly with a man.

"Women continually seek the majority of their passion through men—an unfair burden on men," says James, author of *Women and the Blues: Passions That Hurt, Passions That Heal.*

She urges women to focus on a more sustaining passion—that which comes from doing what they love.

Men seek their passion, she noted, through work, sports, and the world. Most don't expect women to supply all their excitement.

Women must understand that "basic passion comes from your own life and how you live it. If you try to get too much from someone else, you'll always be disappointed," James emphasizes. "It's so important to take responsibility for how exciting your own life is."

In *Women and the Blues*, James cites sources that both women and men can use to create their own passion. The key is finding what thrills you. Consider these suggestions:

Environment. Try planting a garden, hiking in the woods, strolling a beach.

Science. Take a class, read a book, experiment.

Travel. Where have you always wanted to go? Explore a different culture—or a different part of town.

People. Renew a friendship or begin a new one. Make time for friends.

Music. Learn to play an instrument, go to a concert, buy or borrow music new to you.

Animals. Adopt a pet, breed animals, go bird-watching.

Farming. Grow some of your own food; get to know those who do.

Sports. Learn what your body can do. Take a class, attend a game.

Arts and crafts. Create your own, browse galleries and museums, buy or borrow something for display.

Children. Spend more time with your own children or grandchildren, or get to know someone else's.

Writing. Write an autobiography, shape your feelings into poems, write an overdue letter.

Mechanics. Take a car-care class, learn how to do home repairs.

Spirituality. Discover the difference between religion and spirituality. Give your church another chance, or shop around for one that suits you.

Among the impediments to passion, James points out, are fear, need for control, lack of self-value, and being out of touch with ourselves.

What have you loved in the past? What have you always wanted to try or to be or to do? Now pick a passion.

TRUSTING INTUITION

Extrasensory perception: Somehow "knowing" without using the five physical senses—and not being able to explain why.

We've all had psychic experiences: Knowing instinctively that we shouldn't trust someone—and later learning we were right. Feeling compelled to check the baby's room—and discovering a blanket has fallen on the heater. Having a little voice in our heads insist we take an action that gets us just what we needed. Sensing all day that something is wrong with someone we're close to—then getting a call confirming it.

We call them hunches. Gut feelings. Instinct. Women's intuition. A sixth sense.

And we could have more such experiences if we'd stop talking ourselves out of them and work at developing our skills.

It only makes sense, figures Peter Sanders Jr., an honors grad from Massachusetts Institute of Technology who majored in biomedical chemistry with a minor in brain science. Why just use our five physical senses—hearing, sight, taste, touch, and smell—when we have psychic senses as well? he asks.

He defines four psychic senses:

Hearing. This may be a voice in our head, or a more subtle directive. The message is in words or phrases.

Feeling. This is the "gut feeling" we get in the pit of our stomach. (It's different from the adrenalin spurt from fear, which is more a tightening of the chest.)

Vision. These are mental pictures or images that are sometimes like dreaming but without being asleep.

Intuition. This is a sudden knowing, a flash that's there and gone. It's quicker than feeling. We just know, even though we can't explain why.

Many people are afraid of things psychic because we don't understand it. We don't understand it because we can't explain it; it seems spooky, occult, even addlepated. Yet most of us don't understand how our TVs or microwaves work, but that doesn't stop us from using and enjoying them.

"Most people think ESP is only about outlandish things, like when California is going to fall into the ocean, or who Burt Reynolds is going to marry next," says Sanders, a psychic educator.

In 1980 he founded the nonprofit Free Soul in Sedona, Arizona, to help people develop their psychic skills. He's the author of *You Are Psychic!*

Typically when we want to do better at something, we focus on it and concentrate intensely. Tuning in to our psychic senses demands a lighter touch, Sanders says.

That's why he incorporates relaxation techniques into his workshops, because overworked, stressed-out people have trouble tuning in. It's like driving a car under power lines and having the radio go static.

If we couple our unseen senses with the seeing and hearing we use daily, Sanders says, we can get better at perceiving the safety of strangers. Sensing the right approach in business. Knowing when a lover is being fully honest. Finding creative ways to cope with the demands of parenting. Even selecting a reliable baby-sitter.

Sanders purposely engenders ESP in his kids. He travels a lot, so he encourages them to listen for the I-love-you's he beams their way. If they get a hunch, he encourages them to follow up on it and check it out rather than simply dismissing it. He suggests that parents play psychic hide-and-seek. Tell your kids, "You know how Mommy or Daddy feels; just move toward the feeling."

Then hide and let them find you. This will help encourage trust in their own instinct—something many of us spend big bucks on in counseling, workshops, and self-help books.

To sum it all up: Trust yourself.

Are you stumbling through a divorce or grieving a death? Yearning to change careers or agonizing over problems at work? Preparing for parenthood or suffering a mid-life crisis?

No matter what the crisis or transition, you'd do well to sleep on it. To sleep, perchance to dream.

Dreams are X-rays of our subconscious, says California psychologist Alan Siegel, a dream specialist and the author of *Dreams That Can Change Your Life*.

Dreams, Siegel says, are pictures of your feelings about past and present events. Often people repress those feelings while awake, so they come along in sleep and demand attention. Nightmares are feelings screaming for attention. So is having the same dream over and over.

Whether or not you remember your dreams, everyone has four to six dreams per night, or about 150,000 dreams in a lifetime.

In troubled times, people dream even more, starting sixty minutes into sleep instead of the usual ninety minutes, according to studies of people undergoing divorce. The dreams are also more vivid. Nightmares tell you when you're really out of balance.

It's as if the psyche is taking extra time to work on solutions to the problem—just as babies between twelve and eighteen months dream a great deal. Scientists now know that babies are actually programming their brains with all they are learning. That's why when people are learning to drive or to do a new job, they dream about it; they're preparing and practicing.

So what do dreams have to do with relating to yourself and others? Everything.

"Dreams monitor relationships more than anything else—which means our emotional survival, since relationships are so essential to us," says Siegel.

He concurs with Carl Jung that dreams make people whole, giving back ignored or repressed feelings they're not otherwise aware of.

....

"Dreaming is our mind's attempt to survive, to heal our wounds and reach a higher level of awareness and fulfillment," Siegel says.

So how do you get at this snorehouse of goodies?

First, Siegel says, give up some misconceptions:

Misconception: I can't remember my dreams.

Fact: You can train yourself to do so. Remembering them is easier when you're interested in them. Writing them down and talking about them upon awakening helps capture them.

Misconception: My dreams are confusing fragments, not intelligible story lines.

Fact: Dreams don't have to read like fairy tales to be valuable. You can work with funny bits and pieces, and gradually see a pattern emerge.

Misconception: I don't know anything about dream symbols, so I can't analyze my dreams.

Fact: You don't have to be an expert, merely an observer, since dreams are simply pictures of feelings. There's no perfect interpretation of a dream, but there's a collage of possibilities. You see what rings true for you.

Misconception: My dreams were weird because of what I ate.

Fact: Siegel calls that the "burrito theory." Yes, dreams can reflect what's happening in your body, but they still reflect your feelings.

The same types of dreams come to people during transitions. Here are some common themes:

Giving birth to fish or animals. Pregnant women do this: little fish in the first three months, fuzzy animals in the last three months—the creatures get larger as the pregnancy progresses. They may also dream that they forget where their newborn is. Expectant fathers also have baby and birth dreams.

Being alone, isolated, and having no other people in the dream, such as being stranded on a desert island. This is common during divorce as people make the transition from being a couple to being single. One woman dreamed she was riding a unicycle in a crowd of folks on double wheelers.

Nakedness or inadequate or inappropriate clothing. This happens during many transitions when people aren't sure of their identity in a new situation.

Your own death or the death of others close to you. This happens often in mid-life as people confront the death of youthful ideals and the end of a limitless future.

Natural disasters like earthquakes, floods, tornadoes, or buildings collapsing. These dreams occur during all transitions as an old way crumbles. People usually dream of the type of disaster most likely to occur in their area.

Paying attention to your dreams, writing them down, and talking about them can help you understand how you're feeling about something and the progress you're making in dealing with a trauma. Dreams can even provide creative solutions to problems.

Siegel recommends keeping a dream journal and jotting dreams down first thing in the morning. It's not only valuable for keeping in touch with yourself, but it also makes fun reading.

FEAR OF SUCCESS

Success.

We claim to want it, yet we sabotage success in countless ways: We procrastinate. We talk ideas to death instead of doing them. We never quite finish a project.

Many of us stave off success because, deep down, we feel we're not worthy.

Then sometimes, almost in spite of ourselves, success arrives on our front porch. It's rather like having a baby: You know it's going to happen, you plan for it, dream of it—and then suddenly it's there, real— and you can't believe it.

Success can feel scary, almost like a shameful secret. Success carries a whole new set of fears: of being rejected by people, of having our parade rained upon, of having our success somehow invalidated or even ripped away from us overnight. Success can feel good and bad at the same time.

Where does this come from? Many of us get mixed messages about success while growing up.

We did in my family. On the one hand, we were urged to do our best, to do everything perfectly, to finish whatever we began. Those were the words we heard.

The actions we saw told us otherwise. People who did well—especially our more well-to-do relatives—were constantly criticized. My dad started big projects and seldom finished them. Mom pointed out all the reasons something wouldn't work.

So while we were encouraged to succeed, we also were discouraged—not because our parents wanted to confuse us, but because they'd internalized the same messages. Mom was taught in her youth not to try. Dad was extremely poor as a kid; being around people who were better off seemed to trigger feelings of inferiority.

We, too, became the poor relatives, ripping open with both excitement and shame the care packages of clothes handed down from our older cousins. We learned it wasn't nice to talk about money, taking on the shame of our parents.

We also learned to be hypercritical of others, quick to find the flaw to elevate ourselves on the self-worth totem pole.

Through all of this, I defined people as either "haves" and "have-nots." I, of course, was a have-not, and therefore inferior to others. I not only wasn't capable of success, I didn't deserve to have it. I was a perpetual victim, always yearning and never having.

One of my dreams has been to write a book, and when I wrote and sold *Codependent for Sure!* my delight was tempered by fear.

If I flipped suddenly from have-not to have, would people withdraw their friendship? Would they see me as something I wasn't and expect me to be impossibly perfect? Could self-esteem or money or celebrity be snatched away overnight? Did I really deserve success?

It's taken work to correct my faulty thinking about all this. Gradually, these truths emerged:

- It's OK to make mistakes. Everyone does. That's how we learn: through a process of elimination.
- Comparing ourselves to others isn't constructive. And knocking someone else down to feel better about ourselves produces only temporary self-esteem.
- One—or even ten—rejections doesn't mean your idea (or you) is no good. Sometimes it's just a matter of timing.
- Dividing people into categories of have and have-not is simplistic and inaccurate. Contrary to appearances, nobody "has it made." We all have our worries and insecurities.
- We all deserve success—especially when we've worked hard for it.
- Success has many definitions. We each must decide what it means to us. Peace of mind may not be flashy, but it's probably more important than driving a status-symbol car.

What is *your* dream of success? How are you getting in your way?

A Little Girl's Dream

The promise was a long time keeping. But then, so was the dream.

In the early '50s in a small Southern California town, a little girl hefted yet another load of books onto the tiny library's counter.

The girl was a reader. Her parents had books all over their home, but not always the ones she wanted. So she'd make her weekly trek to the yellow library with the brown trim—the little one-room building where the children's library actually was just a nook. Frequently, she ventured out of that nook in search of heftier fare.

As the white-haired librarian hand-stamped the due dates in the ten-year-old's choices, the little girl looked longingly at "The New Book" prominently displayed on the counter. She marveled again at the wonder of writing a book and having it honored like that, right there for the world to see.

That particular day, she confessed her goal. "When I grow up," she said, "I'm going to be a writer. I'm going to write books."

The librarian looked up from her stamping and smiled. Not with the condescension so many children receive, but with encouragement.

"When you do write that book," she replied, "bring it into our library and we'll put it on display, right here on the counter."

The little girl promised she would.

As she grew, so did her dream. She got her first job in ninth grade, writing brief personality profiles, which earned her $1.50 each from the local newspaper. The money paled in comparison with the magic of seeing her words on paper.

A book was a long way off.

She edited her high school paper, married, and started a family, but the itch to write burned deep. She got a part-time job covering school news at a weekly newspaper. It kept her brain busy as she balanced babies.

But no book.

She went to work full time for a major daily. She even tried her hand at magazines.

Still no book.

Finally, she believed she had something to say and started a book. She sent it off to two publishers and was rejected. She put it away, sadly. Several years later, the old dream increasing in persistence, she got an agent and wrote another book. She pulled the other out of hiding, and soon both were sold.

But the world of book publishing moves slower than that of daily newspapers, and she waited two long years. The day the box arrived on her doorstep with its free author's copies, she ripped it open. Then she cried.

She'd waited so long to hold her dream in her hands.

Then she remembered the librarian's invitation, and her promise.

Of course, that particular librarian had died long ago, and the little library had been razed to make way for a larger incarnation.

She called and got the name of the head librarian. She wrote a letter, telling her how much her predecessor's words had meant to the girl. She'd be in town for her thirtieth high school reunion, she wrote, and could she please bring her two books by and give them to the library? It would mean so much to that ten-year-old girl, and it seemed a way of honoring all the librarians who had ever encouraged a child.

The librarian called and said, "Come." So she did, clutching a copy of each book.

She found the big new library right across the street from her old high school—just opposite the room where she'd struggled through algebra, mourning the necessity of a subject that writers would surely never use, and nearly on top of the spot where her old house once stood, the neighborhood having been demolished for a civic center and this looming library.

Inside, the librarian welcomed her warmly. She introduced a reporter from the local newspaper—a descendant of the paper she'd begged a chance to write for long ago.

Then she presented her books to the librarian, who placed them on the counter with a sign of explanation. Tears rolled down the woman's cheeks.

Then she hugged the librarian and left, pausing for a picture outside, which proved that dreams can come true and promises can be kept. Even if it takes thirty-eight years.

The ten-year-old girl and the writer she'd become posed by the library sign. Right next to the readerboard, which said: WELCOME BACK, JANN MITCHELL.

There's a P.S. to that little girl's story. A column I wrote about this experience was selected for the anthology *A Second Helping of Chicken Soup for the Soul*; other columns have been included in other anthologies and even a college human-behavior text. And the book you hold in your hands is the "little girl's" third!

....

What dream awaits *you*? Let your creative juices begin to flow, and it may come true.

14. WONDERFUL WEEKENDS

And on the seventh day, God rested.
—Genesis

"Thank God it's Friday!" or "I've got the Monday blues." How many times have you heard it—or said it?

We seem to spend much of our lives waiting for the weekend, hurrying through five days so that we may enjoy two.

Problem is, we aren't necessarily enjoying those two days. Saturday and Sunday tend to fill up with errands, chores, and activities we can't stuff into the five workdays. Or if we do find time to play, we tend to make it into work.

The phenomenon is examined in *Waiting for the Weekend*, by Witold Rybczynski. The author details the origins of the weekend, which evolved from workers taking Monday off because they were recovering from Sunday's revelry. Eventually, employers gave them Saturday off, with the expectation they'd report to work on Monday as usual.

Rybczynski also delves into some interesting speculation on why the weekend is so darn busy. Having Saturday or Sunday off, he agrees, doesn't feel as delicious as a Tuesday or a Wednesday off.

"If you have to take Saturday off, it's not your free choice. When you decide you're going to take a Wednesday off, it's attractive because you've made the choice—like playing hooky. You're in control."

Rybczynski suggests we distinguish between leisure and recreation, and put some of both into each day.

He sees leisure as more relaxed, less driven, more introspective. We need that during our free time, rather than focusing all our energy onto recreation. If we race from jogging to antiquing, we can fill our time just as much as we do during the workweek.

Our weekends needn't consist solely of either leisure or recreation but are truly balanced when we have some of both.

MAKING WEEKENDS MORE REFRESHING

Here are several ways to create more time for fun during the weekend:

- Incorporate chores and errands into the workweek. Instead of saving it all up for Saturday, do a chore or two before or after work. Get up earlier to run errands, or do them during lunch hour (take clothes to the dry cleaner, shop for a birthday gift). Grocery shop on the way home.

- Trade chores with a partner. If you have a partner or housemates, help each other by trading chores: I'll do your jobs this

Saturday if you'll do mine next weekend. This gives you a truly free weekend. Two-parent families may want to exchange chauffeuring and game-watching duties; Dad can watch junior play soccer this Saturday while Mom does whatever she wants, and vice versa next weekend.

- Do something different during the weekend. Instead of the same old routine such as dinner and a movie Friday night, house-cleaning and errands Saturday, and brunch Sunday, do something completely different. Catch an early (and cheap) movie Saturday or Sunday afternoon, take a drive in the country and have lunch, take off early Saturday morning and leave the chores until later.

- Spend the weekend in your robe and don't leave the house. Do nothing. Not even getting dressed will help you resist the urge to wash the car. Unplug the phone. Watch old movies. Read trashy novels and outlandish tabloids. Eat things that aren't good for you. When people ask what you did all weekend, say, "Nothing," and don't answer when they ask why you're smiling.

- Make no commitments or plans for at least one weekend a month. Do whatever you feel like, as the mood strikes. Rediscover spontaneity. Live the weekend by whim.

- Make an out-of-town trip one weekend a month. Make reservations at a little hideaway for Friday and Saturday and leave right after work. Or just start out driving and see where you end up.

So what are you doing the rest of the weekend?

Making Sundays Special Again

Florence Henderson used to sing a song about "Sunday, sweet Sunday, with nothing to do ...."

It spoke of a simpler time when Sunday was a special day. You could tell Sunday from any other day, whether you were a churchgoer or not.

Stores and other businesses were closed. Families took Sunday drives. We either went to church or slept in and then awakened to a big breakfast. (Surely it was Sunday that gave the world brunch.) We lingered over the thick Sunday paper, the comics spread over the floor.

We trooped to Gramma's for a Sunday dinner—leg of lamb with mint jelly! Dad was home to play with the kids. Relatives and friends were more likely to drop by on this day, and Sunday dinner at home was always more special—fried chicken instead of tuna over toast.

Sunday had a feeling all its own. Leisurely. Quiet, even sleepy. Family-oriented. Special. Even sacred, depending on your religious beliefs.

So what's happened? You can't distinguish it from any other day: Cars clog the mall parking lots. Businesses are not only open Sundays but grocery stores are open all night. Saturday's many errands spill over into Sunday. How many of today's tots have been on a Sunday drive? How many even know that families once sat down together—and without the TV on?

I think we've lost something. If God rested on the seventh day, maybe we should follow suit. Christians who follow a very traditional Sabbath and Jews who observe Shabbat can set an example for us all, no matter what our religious views, reminding us to set aside a day on the weekend to cease work, enjoy family, and remember what's most important.

Here are some things we can do to make Sundays (or Saturdays) special again:

- Declare it to be a work-free day. No housework, no papers from the office, no errands. If you're a business owner or you work at home, rethink your work hours. Rest. Recreate.

- Reinstitute the Sunday drive. Take back roads. Bring a picnic. Discover places you've never seen. Sing songs and stop wherever you want. The children may complain at first, but they'll have happy family memories in years to come. Or get a sitter and enjoy time alone with your spouse or a friend. Get lost, so you can get found.

- Stay out of stores and enjoy the outdoors. Bike through the neighborhood. Hike in the woods. Amble down a beach. Move slowly, and truly see.

- Do only what you enjoy today. No shoulds or oughts—only wants.

- Bring back the Sunday dinner, with food that takes time (and love) to prepare. Let everyone sit down together, with no TV. Invite in family or friends.

- Attend services at a church or synagogue, or follow another spiritual practice that puts you in touch with the power of the universe. Meditate, be alone in nature, write in your journal, wonder about what it all means.

- Take the phone off the hook, unplug the TV, and disconnect from the world. Make a fire, read, write letters, listen to music, think deep thoughts.

- Declare it (or at least part of it) to be Family Day. No one runs off to do their own thing, holes up in their room, or hides behind earphones. Talk to each other, play games, work on a fun project together, join in preparing a meal, or just hang out.
- Begin a tradition: Breakfast in bed with the newspaper, brunch out, dinner at Gramma's, an afternoon movie, an evening potluck with friends, popcorn and board games, a family walk in the rain or snow or sunshine.

Think back to your own childhood: What made Sunday memorable? How can you incorporate that into your life today?

Let's make Sunday (or Saturday) a day to savor again.

15. Soul Sustenance

We have to decide for ourselves what's nourishing to our souls, and do those things over others.
—Thomas Moore

Like love, souls require nurturing. They must be honored and fed. Our souls are the spiritual seat of the self. Ignore the soul and all life seems shallow; we feel disconnected from the universe.

We can nurture our souls in many ways. Here are a few of them.

Inspiring Spirituality

For me, spirituality is connectedness—with myself, others, nature, and the power of the universe, which is larger and more enduring than us all.

What comprises spirituality differs among people. For some, church every Sunday is a must. Others haven't set foot in one for years, yet they "worship" daily through their acute appreciation of everyday life.

Looking at what others do can help us shape our own form of spirituality. This is what works for me.

CONNECTION WITH OTHERS

- Letting those I love know it, freely and frequently.
- Truly connecting each day with a co-worker or friend and sharing something meaningful, not just gossip.
- Spending time with children, to see with fresh eyes.
- Sharing what I've learned and who I am—which means sometimes risking and revealing myself, knowing that others have been there, too. We are not alone in our pain, our joy, our frustration.
- Having a mission statement to keep me focused on my values and to ward off the unimportant.
- Shopping at farmers' and crafts markets to talk with the person who grew or made the product.
- Understanding those who came before as I grow older, savoring that connection, and passing it on to my children and grandchildren through family stories and photos.
- Seeing the commonalities in all people rather than just the differences.

SOLITUDE

- Meditating—simply sitting in receptive silence, knowing that while prayer is talking to God, meditation is listening.

- Writing in my journal to check in with myself.

- Scheduling time alone onto my calendar.

- Doing nothing but staring into space.

- Asking, "What now, God?"

AN ATTITUDE OF GRATITUDE

- Taking walks to see the beautiful, humorous, or touching.

- Accepting and appreciating my body.

- Understanding that the ordinariness of today will become the "good old days" of next year or the next decade.

- Focusing on the positive rather than the negative.

- Sprinkling humor and play throughout my day.

- Choosing books, movies, and music which uplift rather than depress me or degrade others.

- Being with people who are supportive and inspiring.

- Surrounding myself with beauty—flowers on my desk, candles at dinner.

- Trying to do the right thing, whether it's picking up a piece of litter off the street or giving up a long-nurtured resentment.

BEING IN NATURE

- Taking to the woods whenever possible.

- Watching the birds at my feeder, the squirrels in the trees.

- Lying in bed and watching the trees shed their fall finery, the clouds scud by, the rain dapple the pond.

- Growing plants or herbs on my deck, moving them inside before the frost hits.
- Going to U-pick fruit and vegetable farms.
- Walking the beach and feeling the power of the sea.

MAINTAINING PERSPECTIVE

- Remembering that "This, too, shall pass."
- Knowing that relationships—not things—bring happiness.
- Keeping in mind that each setback, each disappointment, even each tragedy, holds a lesson and an opportunity for me. It's my job to find it.
- Appreciating that the world does not revolve around me—but that I have a place in it, with my own unique contributions to make.

As children, most of us feel a natural connection to the universe. Some of us have that educated out of us in one way or another.

Once we get it back, we can feel more whole. Not alone. Connected to all those who came before, those with whom we share our planet now, and those who will come after.

What form does your spirituality take?

BLESSINGS IN BED—ALONE!

Talk about bed and the first things that come to mind are sleep and sex. And maybe insomnia.

We spend about a third of our lives in bed. But when we're asleep or romantically involved, we're really not conscious of the simple pleasures that bed can bring. I once spent nearly a month recuperating from pneumonia—lots of time to muse on ways to savor the sack.

Here are some soul-nurturing satisfying ways to spend time in bed:

- After a tough day, pamper yourself. Slip into your jammies, fix breakfast for dinner, and crawl into bed to enjoy it.

- Make phone calls. Lying down is much more comfortable for pleasant chats. If you're calling long-distance, you may want to set your alarm clock so you don't lose track of the time.

- At the first sign of a cold or flu, get into bed after fixing yourself a cup of hot lemonade with honey. It felt better when Mom did it, but if she's no longer around, plug in the heating pad, rub Vicks on your chest, and put the pad on your chest (over an old T-shirt).

- Do school homework, projects brought home from the office, or craft work. There's plenty of space to spread out your books, papers, and supplies, and it may be the warmest place in a drafty apartment. Be careful not to fall asleep!

- Bed can also be therapeutic. It's the best place in the world to feel sorry for yourself. Throw yourself on it, flail your arms and legs, and have a good cry. Read old love letters, sort through the cards from the funeral, sob into your pillow so no one else can hear. Pull the covers over your head and shut out the world for a while.

- Take your therapy a little further: beat on your mattress with a bat, stick, rolling pin, or broom, and work out all your anger and frustrations. The bed can't hit back and no one will be hurt—and you'll feel a lot better.

- Plan a vacation. When the wind is howling outside, it's delicious to be tucked beneath a down comforter littered with maps and travel brochures from sunny climes.
- Write letters and Christmas cards. Be careful not to set your pen down and get ink on the sheets.
- On a blustery weekend, stay in bed all day. Read, snooze, snack, watch a movie.
- Be a kid again. Prop yourself up and read comics or a favorite childhood novel. (I recently enjoyed rereading *The Wizard of Oz* from the original book I received at age eight.) Color or connect the dots. Cut out paper dolls or make paper airplanes. Watch TV cartoons.
- Entertain. My grandmother told about a zany friend who came calling when Gramma had taken to bed with depression. Her friend climbed right in, feathered hat and all. During my recent bout, my small grandson spent a happy hour in bed with me as we fashioned Halloween ghosts with tissues over Tootsie-Pops. He had a bad cold, so we both sipped cups of hot lemonade and called ourselves "sickies making ghosties."

How well do you like your bed? Is it a flat spot to flop or a privileged perch?

A year ago, I bought my dream bed: thick pine logs, whitewashed to match the Southwestern decor. It's big and high and sturdy—a bed to give birth in or die in, a pampered-guest-at-a-bed-and-breakfast kind of bed.

Topping it off is a down comforter—a European vacation convinced me to splurge. Sewing two coordinating sheets together for a comforter cover gave me an inexpensive, reversible ensemble to coordinate with sheets (cozy flannel in winter). Two sets of bed pillows and a throw pillow or two make it so divine it's a shame when the alarm rings.

Bedtime at any time is more enjoyable with the curtains open to enjoy the falling leaves, darting birds, and scudding clouds—and the window ajar for fresh air. It also helps to keep the bedroom tidy with things you enjoy looking at. Add a good reading light, a bedstand with the essentials, and a pile of books, and you may never get up.

If you're reading this in bed, you're probably already a sack slug. It's one of the little joys in life, isn't it?

TRY A HOME RETREAT

Can't afford to cruise the Nile, shop in Soho, or trek the Himalayas?

Take a home retreat whenever you feel the need of a vacation. All it requires is time off work or daily responsibilities and a respite from the niggling work ethic that says you should feel guilty if you're not being productive.

The idea is to do what you want to when you want to. Don't fill up all your leisure time with projects. Try letting the housework go until the last day.

HOLE UP

Hide out in your little cocoon and try the following ideas:

- Rent your favorite videos, draw the drapes, and make a bowl of popcorn.

- Put on your favorite records or tapes and sing along.

- Take a bubble bath in candlelight.

- Get out your old high school yearbook or old love letters and moon over them. Share 'em with your kids to prove you really were young once.

- Take a break from self-improvement or required reading and curl up with an engrossing novel.

- Unplug your phone and sleep.

- Start keeping a journal, or make a scrapbook of your life.

- Make a dream list of places you want to go and things you want to do.

- Work on your hobby as long as you want; leave all the stuff out until tomorrow.

DO SOMETHING DIFFERENT

Break from your rest-of-the-year routine:

- Try an ethnic restaurant. (Go for lunch—it'll be cheaper than dinner.)

- Hit the museum, historical society, or art galleries in your town. Thomas Moore assures us that's "not being artsy-fartsy. It's like looking into a mirror—art says something about our lives. It's looking at images that present to us insight into the great mysteries and puzzles of human existence: aggression, beauty, love." Dreams, he adds, are a personal art gallery.

- Cook ahead a few days, then dine on salads and cold cuts. Use paper plates to avoid washing dishes.

- Go to an afternoon movie at discount prices.
- Meet a friend for a three-hour lunch.
- Redecorate your bedroom.
- Go to the library and read magazines for free.
- Browse the shops in a section of town you don't usually frequent.
- Go roller-skating. You'll feel you're in eighth grade again.
- Spook around a costume shop and plan what to be for Halloween.
- Check out a church or temple if you never go—or a different one from your usual place of worship.
- Invite friends over for a potluck barbecue.

GET OUTDOORS

Take advantage of the weather (or brave a blustery day) and go outside:

- Head for the river with a picnic. Swim, skip rocks, fish, sun, make sandcastles.
- Go for a hike in a park or head for the hills.
- Attend a county or state fair.
- Walk through your neighborhood and talk to folks you don't know.
- Build a tree house or backyard fort with the kids.
- String a hammock between two trees or poles and take a load off.
- Take a bus to the end of its route. Get out and walk around before you head for home.
- Take a picnic and head for a park—or an outdoor concert, play, or pageant.

- Work on your tan (sparingly—and avoid the noonday sun).

- Make a day trip to the beach, the mountains, down the valley.

- Go for a swim at the lake, river, or local pool.

- Attend a local festival or arts-and-crafts show.

- Set up the barbecue and see how many meals can be prepared outdoors.

If You Must Work

If you get bored and insist on doing something productive, do something that rests your brain:

- Paint the fence. Reserve one section for handprints of the kids or friends and relatives.

- Muck out a closet and pitch the stuff you haven't used in months or years. (Donate it to charity and take a tax deduction.)

- Write letters you owe.

- Get caught up on your photo albums.

- Straighten up the garage, attic, or basement.

- Weed the garden or start a new one in containers.

- Clean out your bookshelf and take the discards to a used bookstore for resale.

With Some Loose Change

Got a little money put ahead by staying at home? Treat yourself:

- Splurge at an expensive restaurant.

- Book a river cruise.

- Check into a bed-and-breakfast or hotel for one night; enjoy breakfast in bed.
- Go on a shopping spree for something you've always wanted.
- Attend a play or concert.

If you don't recharge your batteries, who will?

KEEPING A JOURNAL

Not many things are (1) free, (2) sometimes fun and sometimes painful, (3) able to improve your relationship with yourself and others, (4) done in private, and (5) like seeing a therapist without leaving home.

But that's what keeping a journal can do.

Entire books have been written on the subject, but journal-keeping doesn't have to be that difficult.

Write whenever you feel like it; it needn't be a daily chore. Chronicling what you're doing is less important than writing down how you feel about what's happening in your life.

The purpose is to get to know yourself better, to have a private place to ruminate on your fantasies and torments, to explore the problems and puzzles of living.

And if you ever wonder if you're making any personal progress at all, a browse through past journals will prove that you are. Right there in your own handwriting are all the angst and problems that somehow resolved themselves—often despite your worry and attempts to control.

Use a pretty, fabric-covered journal with lined or blank pages, a spiral notebook, or a loose-leaf binder. Some people keep journals on their computers, but I prefer to curl up with mine, and I enjoy their bright spots of color as they accrue in my bedroom. Here are some suggestions for getting started in keeping a journal. Most of them are lists—they're easy to write, and they can be added to at any time.

Remember, no one will grade your journal. There's no "right way" to do it. No one's peeking over your shoulder. It's just for you.

KNOWING YOURSELF BETTER

- List things and qualities that your perfect dream room might have.
- List places you'd like to visit.
- List things you're afraid of and why.
- List things you'd like to have done when you die.
- List things you hate, and things you love.
- List fantasies you have.
- List aspects of yourself you'd like to work on.
- List books you'd like to read, or those you've especially enjoyed, or subjects you'd like to learn more about.
- Record your dreams and decipher their message.
- Devise a "I know I'm lapsing when I..." list for warning signs that you're falling back into victim-thinking, compulsive behavior, worrying too much, relying on others for self-esteem, etc.
- List things you want. (Share your list at birthday, Christmas, and anniversary times.)

- List significant memories—good and bad—from childhood. How do they affect you today?

FEELING BETTER ABOUT YOURSELF

- Write down compliments you receive.
- List things you're proud of.
- List what you like about yourself.
- List things you've done in your life (positive, negative, neutral— just what you've done and experienced).
- List what you've learned since you married, got divorced, became a parent, left home, entered therapy, etc.
- List goals you have and what small steps you can begin taking to reach them.
- List things, places, and people you enjoy. Arrange to enjoy at least one of them daily or weekly.

DEALING WITH OTHERS

- List the people you clash with most. What do they have in common? What buttons do they push? How are you alike?
- List resentments you hold. What can you do about them?
- List the qualities that attracted you to your partner—and review these when times get tough.
- List the qualities most important to you in a relationship. How does your relationship stack up?

- If you've broken up recently, list the reasons you left—and refer to them when you're tempted to call or contact that person.
- List the qualities you appreciate in each child; list the characteristics that concern you. List ways you can encourage and help each child.
- List the positive and negative aspects of each of your parents. Which traits do you want to keep in yourself? Which do you want to guard against?
- List your loved ones' hints or requests about things they want. Refer to them when it's time to buy a gift.

And if you're ever famous, just think how much these journals will be worth!

HAVE A MASSAGE

What do you do when you're stressed, stiff, out of sorts, and out of touch?

Some of us snap on the TV, reach for a drink, open the fridge, or go shopping. Others of us pick up the phone and make an appointment for a massage.

Call it a gift to ourself.

A professional massage not only feels great, but it offers lots of little life lessons.

Massage offers many opportunities to help us:

Nurture ourselves. Massage is physically and emotionally beneficial, without the harmful effects of many feel-better solutions. It's a way of being good to ourselves.

Receive without having to give. This sounds ideal, but for many of us, it's easier to give than to receive, because that way we feel more in control and can even obligate another person to us.

Set boundaries. We can say to the massage therapist, "I'm comfortable being touched there, but please don't touch me here." It is especially important to sexual-abuse survivors to be able—finally—to say this, and to feel safe being touched. A professional honors our feelings.

Have a sensual experience in a safe, professional setting. There's no need to run the risk of hit-and-run lovers to have an adventure. Every massage therapist's style is different, so it's always fun to see how the massage will be this time.

Ask for what we need. We can say, "My neck and shoulders are where I carry tension. Please give them extra attention."

Set limits. We can set the tone of the massage, saying, "No, that hurts. I want a lighter touch, please." This is good practice for stating needs during lovemaking. We can practice with a safe massage therapist whose feelings we don't feel compelled to protect. If at any point we don't feel comfortable, we can say so—or even stop the massage.

Enjoy our bodies and rediscover sensation. For those of us who live in our heads, getting back in touch with our bodies is necessary for balance and for any healing work we may be doing. Massage lets us feel sensation in a nonsexual way.

Surrender in a safe atmosphere. Feeling safe, we can relinquish control and vigilance and let ourselves relax. Many people—especially people who were abused by a member of the opposite sex—feel more comfortable getting a massage from someone of the same gender. You can specify whether you prefer a man or woman.

Practice peace from the inside out. If we often try to make external circumstances perfect before we can feel peaceful, here's the chance to turn things around. During my most recent massage, construction in another room created a distraction, but eventually I got so focused and relaxed that I was able to disregard it.

Let ourselves play. Trusting someone to move our arms and legs and massage even our toes feels playful. I couldn't help adding a "Wee, wee, wee, all the way home" when my masseuse finished my small toe.

Enjoy the warmth and comfort of human touch. All people need touch; newborns wither without it. Massage is especially comforting if our bodies or souls are in pain, or if we aren't regularly or lovingly touched by a lover. The touch and closeness of a massage therapist can make us feel like a child again, safe and loved in our mother's lap.

Make decisions and discoveries about what we like and don't like. Listening to our bodies during massage can help us trust them in other circumstances as well. (For instance, if we're aware of our stomachs knotting up whenever our spouse or boss approaches, that's information we need to know.) Our bodies feel safe with a person, or they don't. This time we can acknowledge and act on what our bodies tell us.

Reduce the pain of abuse by providing loving touch. If others have abused our bodies through childhood beatings, neglect, or sexual abuse, or if we have abused them through eating too much or too little, smoking, drinking too much, using drugs, or not exercising, massage makes amends. It says, "I'm sorry for what happened to you, and I will see that you are loved and taken care of."

Find a massage therapist you like by asking friends who've had massages, getting referrals from health professionals or your local Y, or browsing through the Yellow Pages or the classifieds in health- or recovery-related publications. Massages are usually given in half-hour or hour increments; your trunk is kept covered by a sheet. Prices vary. Think of massage as an investment in your physical and emotional well-being. Preventive medicine. A gift to yourself. Something you deserve.

Aye, there's the rub.

BIRTHDAY BLESSINGS

How do you feel about that next birthday coming up—or the one you just celebrated: Ancient? Over the hill? Depressed? Impossible to believe you made it this far?

Do you glory in racking up another year of living? Feel a little wiser? Grateful for another spin through the seasons? Proud of those little laugh lines around your eyes and mouth?

Even more than New Year's, birthdays are important demarcation points—perhaps because they're so personal. After all, a birthday is the day we celebrate *us*.

Yet I wonder just how much celebrating we really do at birthday time. Just look through the card shops at the proliferation of black balloons, "Rest in Peace" placards, and "50 isn't old if you're a tree" T-shirts.

In our youth-worshipping culture, birthdays seem more and more an occasion to mourn rather than to celebrate. We blow birthdays off as an embarrassment, an inconvenience, a milepost closer to the inevitable.

Perhaps we can learn something about birthdays from a small child. Or a terminally ill person. Or someone who's lost a loved one too young. None of these people take a birthday for granted.

How can we make our next birthday less blasé? Here are some suggestions:

Do something symbolic. Pass on the gift of life by giving blood or filling out an organ-donor card. Send flowers or a card of thanks to the one who raised you. (If you're adopted, send a mental note of gratitude to the one who loved you enough to give you a better chance at life.) Donate money to your favorite charity—perhaps a dollar for each year you're celebrating.

Realize a dream. Stop postponing what you want to do. A friend spent her summer birthday rafting a wild river. Perhaps this year you can mark yours on a tropical isle, picnicking in Central Park, or cheering in Dodger Stadium. Or register to go back to school.

Reconnect with the past. One of my best birthdays was spent with my sisters. They made me an angel-food cake, just as my grandmother always had. (I was born on her birthday and we always celebrated together.) My best girlfriend from childhood joined us for lunch. That evening, we enjoyed a barbecue reminiscing with a childhood friend and his family. We recaptured the fun of our youth by staging an impromptu talent show. (We felt like kids again, and the children loved it.)

Give yourself a gift. Doing exactly what I wanted made my fortieth birthday unforgettable. I took the day off work and had a masseuse come to the house. I had lunch alone in a lovely tea room and wrote a few poems. Then I went shopping. Those things alone made it a red-letter day.

Bask in the love of friends. Some of us would rather swim across an icy river in January than be the subject of a surprise party. Others love them. That fortieth birthday got even better when my husband—who was ostensibly taking me to dinner—pulled by a mortuary, saying he had to pay brief respects to a fraternity brother. Inside was a banner reading "Happy 40th, Jann—You look so natural" and a roomful of friends who proceeded to eulogize/roast me. I'd often mused on how interesting it would be to hear what people said at my funeral, so here was my chance. Afterward, we all went for pizza. It was so much fun, I forgot to feel old.

Ask for what you need. I know a thoughtful woman who gives wonderful birthday gifts to others but is seldom remembered by her own husband and children simply because she's never conveyed to them how important birthdays are to her. People who love us aren't mind readers—and some are incredibly slow learners. But they're usually happy to give us what we want if they know what that is. So if you want a surprise party, a nice dinner out, or fancy lingerie instead of a new vacuum cleaner, ask.

Another way to ask for what we need is to throw our own birthday party. Let your friends know it's your special day, invite them over, and enjoy being the center of attention for a few hours. They'll feel good, and you will, too.

Spend time reflecting on your life. A birthday is an appropriate time to look at where you've been and where you'd like to go. You might take that magic number you're turning and list forty things you're grateful for, twenty-five things you're proud of, sixty people you're glad you've known. This may be the time to get a little sentimental: Pore over old photo albums, shed some tears, forgive someone. Then put away the past and anticipate all the wonderful surprises awaiting us.

This year, celebrate the passage of another year with an attitude of gratitude. Rejoice in the hard-learned lessons, joys, and fortitude that brought us to this special day.

And remember the wise words of Jennifer James: "The key to getting older with pleasure is just that—running your own life. If we continue to live by others' expectations, we will age by them, too."

THE HEALING POWER OF VOLUNTEERING

Feeling down? Then do something for somebody else.

Helping others can keep and even help restore good health, according to research published in *The Healing Power of Doing Good*, by Allan Luks with Peggy Payne .

Luks has helped others all his life, from the Peace Corps to the Big Brothers/Big Sisters of New York City.

While Luks knew that helping others had kept him and others healthy, he wanted to prove it. So he expanded on various pieces of medical research, including a 1976 federal study of the Retired Senior Volunteer Program which showed that the physical and mental health of 98 percent of the volunteers over sixty had improved significantly after they began participating in the program.

The author collaborated with Dr. Howard Andrews of the New York State Psychiatric Institute to formulate unbiased questions distributed to 3,300 volunteers at more than twenty volunteer organizations throughout the nation.

Here are the results:

- The majority of volunteers reported less stress and tension as well as a general sense of well-being when they helped others.
- Ninety-five percent reported feeling an immediate "helper's high"— warmth, increased energy, and euphoria.
- An extended feeling of calm, self-worth, and relaxation follows the high.
- These volunteers say they feel better than other people do, and eight of ten say they feel good all over again whenever they think of their volunteer work.
- The more they help, the better they feel. People who help others several times weekly report better health than those who volunteer only once a year.
- Those who feel the best have personal contact with the person being helped and worked with strangers rather than family or friends.
- The healthiest people can let go of the outcome of their helping and simply enjoy the experience.

"How much we accomplish for someone," Luks says, "is not as important as whether we feel a connection, a vicarious experience of the other person's problems, a recognition of him or her as a fellow being.

"These feelings which are transmitted to our bodies produce the good, relaxing sensations that seem to lie at the heart of healthy helping."

Volunteers report improvement in physical maladies ranging from headaches to sensitivity to pain and emotional lows as well as mental and emotional conditions. Katrinka Easterday, director of the Multnomah County, Oregon, Retired and Senior Volunteer Program for people fifty-five and over, says she sees such results daily.

"We see people in walkers, people who've retired or lost a spouse—it's like they died themselves. And we see them flourish, come alive again. It's just phenomenal."

How would you like to become involved in your community?

As Thomas Moore reminds us:

....

"Soul is not about understanding. It's about connecting."

Resources

Organizational Help

To find a professional organizer near you, or to receive brochures on various organizational solutions, contact:

National Association of Professional Organizers
1033 La Posada, Suite 220
Austin, TX 78752
Referral and Information Hotline:
(512) 206-0151, fax (512) 454-3036

Japanese Gardens

Enjoy strolling a Japanese garden in these cities in the United States and Canada: Birmingham, Ala.; Phoenix, Ariz; Auburn, Corona Del Mar, Culver City, Eureka, Glendale, Hayward, Hollywood, La Canada, Lodi, West Los Angeles, Monterey Park, Oakland, San Diego, San Francisco, San Jose, San Marino, San Mateo, Saratoga, Van Nuys, Whittier, Calif.; Denver, Colo.; Washington, D.C.; Delray Beach, Miami, Miami Beach, Fla.; Atlanta, Ga.; Honolulu and Haneohe in Oahu, Kalaheo in Kauai, Hawaii; Decatur, Glencoe, Rockford, Ill.; New Iberia, New Orleans, La.; Northeast Harbor, Maine; Monkton, Md.; Boston, Duxbury, Edgartown, Northampton, Salem, South Hadley, Westfield, Mass.; Midland, Niles, Mich.; Saginaw, Northfield, St. Paul, Minn.; Jackson, Miss.; Lakewood, N.J.; Brooklyn, Bronx, Buffalo, Canandaigua, Mill Neck, Millbrook,

North Salem, Old Westbury, N.Y.; Cleveland, Newark, Oberlin, Shaker Heights, Ohio; Grove, Okla.; Coos Bay, Medford, Portland, Ore.; Bethlehem, Kennett Square, Malvern, Philadelphia, Pa.; Portsmouth, Providence, R.I.; Greenville, S.C.; Memphis, Nashville, Tenn.; Austin, Dallas, Fort Worth, Houston, Texas; Salt Lake City, Utah; Norfolk, Richmond, Va.; Bainbridge Island, Bellevue, Edmonds, Seattle, Spokane, Tacoma, Wash.; Edmonton, Lethbridge, Alberta; New Westminster, Vancouver, Victoria, British Columbia.

PSYCHOLOGICAL ASPECTS OF HOME

House as a Mirror of Self: Exploring the Deeper Meaning of Home, by Clare Cooper Marcus (Conari, 1995).

Where the Heart Is: A Celebration of Home, anthology edited by Julienne Bennett and Mimi Luebbermann (Wildcat Canyon Press, 1995).

FENG SHUI

Feng Shui Made Easy: Designing Your Life with the Ancient Art of Placement, by William Spear (HarperCollins, 1995).

Interior Design with Feng Shui, by Susan Rossbach and Lin Yun (Arkana/Penguin, 1987).

STEPFAMILIES

For information on blended families, or to find or start a support group in your area, contact:

The Stepfamily Association of America, Inc.
215 Centennial Mall So., Suite 212
Lincoln, NE 68508
(402) 477-STEP or 1-800-735-0329

JUNK MAIL

To reduce the amount of junk mail you receive, keep your name off mailing lists. Send your request to these two organizations, listing your address and each variation of your name (Jane Smith, Mrs. Bob Smith, etc.) in which you get junk mail. It will take about six months before you see a difference.

Mail Preference Service
Direct Marketing Association
P.O. Box 9008
Farmingdale, NY 11735-9008

Director of List Maintenance, Advo Inc.
1 Univac Lane
Windsor, CT 06095-0755

SIMPLER LIVING

For a pamphlet on simpler living, send a self-addressed, stamped envelope to:

New Road Map Foundation
P.O. Box 15981
Seattle, WA 98115
(206) 527-0437

For instructions on starting your own support group on simple living and downsizing, send $5.78 for a "Simplicity Circle Guide" to:

Cecile Andrew
711 N. 60th St.
Seattle, WA 98103

Quarterly newsletter, *Simple Living: The Journal of Voluntary Simplicity.* $14 yearly subscription. Write to:

Simple Living Press
2319 N. 45th St., Box 149
Seattle, WA 98103
(206) 464-4800

Monthly newsletter, *Out of the Rat Race: Inspirational and Practical Ideas for Those Who Want to Escape.* $12 yearly subscription. Write to:

Gregory Communications Group
P.O. Box 95341
Seattle, WA 98145-2341

Monthly newsletter, *Simple Living News.* $16 for ten issues yearly. Write to:

Simple Living News
P.O. Box 1884
Jonesboro, GA 30237
(770) 471-9048

Sources and Bibliography

Permissions

The publisher and author gratefully acknowledge and thank the following for permission to use previously published material:

Adler, Margot. *Drawing Down the Moon.* (Boston: Beacon Press.) Copyright © 1986 by Margot Adler. Reprinted by permission of the author.

Baldwin, Christina. *Life's Companion: Journal Writing As a Spiritual Quest.* (New York: Bantam Doubleday Dell.) Copyright © 1990 by Christina Baldwin. Reprinted by permission of the publisher.

Beck, Renee, and Sydney Barbara Metrick. *The Art of Ritual: A Guide to Creating and Performing Your Own Ceremonies for Growth and Change.* (Berkeley, Calif.: Celestial Arts.) Copyright © 1990 by Renee Beck and Sydney Barbara Metrick. Reprinted by permission of the publisher.

Bender, Sue. *Plain and Simple: A Woman's Journey to the Amish.* (New York: HarperCollins.) Copyright © 1989 by Sue Bender. Reprinted by permission of the author.

Bloch, Douglas. *Words That Heal.* (New York: Bantam Books.) Copyright © 1990 by Douglas Bloch. Reprinted by permission of the author.

Bradshaw, John. *Family Secrets: What You Don't Know Can Hurt You.* (New York: Bantam.) Copyright © 1995 by Bantam Books. Reprinted by permission of the author.

Cameron, Julia, with Mark Bryan. *The Artist's Way: A Spiritual Path to Higher Creativity*. (New York: Jeremy P. Tarcher.) Copyright © 1992 by Julia Cameron. Reprinted by permission of the publisher.

De Angelis, Barbara. *Real Moments*. (New York: Bantam Doubleday Dell, Delacorte Press.) Copyright © 1994 by Barbara De Angelis. Reprinted by permission of the author.

Duerk, Judith. *Circle of Stones: A Woman's Journey to Herself*. (San Diego: LuraMedia.) Copyright © 1989 by LuraMedia. Reprinted by permission of the publisher.

Ealy, C Diane. *The Woman's Book of Creativity*. (Hillsboro, Ore.: Beyond Words Publishing.) Copyright © 1995 by C Diane Ealy. Reprinted by permission of the publisher.

Hancock, Emily. *The Girl Within: Recapture the Childhood Self, the Key to Female Identity*. (New York: Penguin USA.) Copyright © 1990 by Penguin USA. Reprinted by permission of the author.

Harris, Maria. *Jubilee Time: Celebrating Women, Spirit, and the Advent of Age*. (New York: Bantam.) Copyright © 1995 by Maria Harris. Reprinted by permission of the publisher.

James, Jennifer. *Success Is the Quality of Your Journey*. (New York: Newmarket Press.) Copyright © 1986 by Jennifer James. Reprinted by permission of the author.

James, Jennifer. *Visions from the Heart*. (Seahurst, Wash.: Bronwen Press.) Copyright © 1991 by Jennifer James. Reprinted by permission of the author.

James, Jennifer. *Women and the Blues: Passions That Hurt, Passions That Heal*. (New York: Harper & Row.) Copyright © 1988 by Jennifer James. Reprinted by permission of the author.

Jeffers, Susan. *Dare to Connect: Reaching Out in Romance, Friendship and the Workplace.* (New York: Ballantine, Fawcett Columbine.) Copyright © 1992 by Susan Jeffers. Reprinted by permission of the author.

Jeffers, Susan. *Feel the Fear and Do It Anyway.* (New York: Ballantine, Fawcett Columbine.) Copyright © 1987 by Susan Jeffers. Reprinted by permission of the author.

Keyes, Ralph. *Timelock: How Life Got So Hectic and What You Can Do About It.* (New York: HarperCollins.) Copyright © 1991 by HarperCollins. Reprinted by permission of the publisher.

Lara, Adair. *Slowing Down in a Speeded Up World.* (Berkeley, Calif.: Conari Press.) Copyright © 1994 by Adair Lara. Reprinted by permission of the publisher.

Louden, Jennifer. *The Woman's Comfort Book: A Self-Nurturing Guide to Restoring Balance in Your Life.* (San Francisco: HarperSanFrancisco.) Copyright © 1992 by Jennifer Louden. Reprinted by permission of the author.

Louv, Richard. *Childhood's Future.* (New York: Doubleday, Anchor.) Copyright © 1992 by Richard Louv. Reprinted by permission of the author.

Luhrs, Janet, editor. *Simple Living: The Journal of Voluntary Simplicity.* (Seattle: Simple Living Press.) Copyright © 1995 by Simple Living Press. Reprinted by permission of the editor.

Luks, Allan, with Peggy Payne. *The Healing Power of Doing Good.* (New York: Ballantine, Fawcett Columbine.) Copyright © 1992 by Allan Luks and Peggy Payne. Reprinted by permission of the author.

Lysne, Robin Heerens. *Dancing up the Moon: A Woman's Guide to Creating Traditions That Bring Sacredness to Daily Life.* (Berkeley, Calif.: Conari Press.) Copyright © 1995 by Robin Heerens Lysne. Reprinted by permission of the publisher.

Moore, Thomas. *Care of the Soul: A Guide for Cultivating Depth and Sacredness in Everyday Life*. (New York: HarperPerennial.) Copyright © 1991 by Thomas Moore. Reprinted by permission of the author.

Moore, Thomas. *Soul Mates: Honoring the Mysteries of Love and Relationship*. (New York: HarperCollins.) Copyright © 1994 by Thomas Moore. Reprinted by permission of the author.

Robin, Vicki, and Joe Dominguez. *Your Money or Your Life: Transforming Your Relationship with Money and Achieving Financial Independence*. (New York: Viking Penguin.) Copyright © 1992 by Vicki Robin and Joe Dominguez. Reprinted by permission of the authors.

Rybczynski, Witold. *Waiting for the Weekend*. (New York: Viking.) Copyright © 1991 by Witold Rybczynski. Reprinted by permission of the author.

Sanders, Peter A., Jr. *You Are Psychic!* (New York: Ballantine, Fawcett Columbine.) Copyright © 1991 by Fawcett Columbine. Reprinted by permission of the author.

Siegel, Alan B. *Dreams That Can Change Your Life: A Guide to Navigating Life's Passages Through Turning Point Dreams*. (New York: Jeremy P. Tarcher.) Copyright © 1991 by Alan B. Siegel. Reprinted by permission of the publisher.

Van Wey, Chantall. *Chantall's Handy-Dandy Do-It-Yourself Visualization Kit*. (Yachats, Ore.: By the Sea Books.) Copyright © 1995 by Chantall Van Wey. Reprinted by permission of the author.

Wall, Steve, and Harvey Arden. *Wisdomkeepers: Meetings with Native American Spiritual Elders*. (Hillsboro, Ore.: Beyond Words Publishing.) Copyright © 1990 by Steve Wall and Harvey Arden. Reprinted by permission of the publisher.

ADDITIONAL BIBLIOGRAPHY

Bepko, Claudia, and Jo-Ann Krestan. *Singing at the Top of Our Lungs: Women, Love, and Creativity.* New York: HarperPerennial, 1994.

Canfield, Jack, and Mark Victor Hansen. *A Second Helping of Chicken Soup for the Soul: 101 More Stories to Open the Heart and Rekindle the Spirit.* Deerfield Beach, Fla.: Health Communications, 1995.

Covey, Stephen. *The Seven Habits of Highly Effective People.* New York: Simon and Schuster, 1990.

Elgin, Duane. *Voluntary Simplicity: Toward a Way of Life That Is Outwardly Simple, Inwardly Rich.* New York: William Morrow, Quill, 1993.

Fitzpatrick, Jean Grasso. *Something More: Nurturing Your Child's Spiritual Growth.* New York: Viking Penguin, 1992.

Klein, Tzipora. *Celebrating Life: Rites of Passage for All Ages.* Oak Park, Ill.: Delphi Press, 1992.

Mitchell, Jann. *Organized Serenity: How to Manage Your Time and Life in Recovery.* Deerfield Beach, Fla.: Health Communications, 1992.

OTHER BOOKS FROM
BEYOND WORDS PUBLISHING, INC.

THE WOMAN'S BOOK OF CREATIVITY
Author: C Diane Ealy, $12.95 softcover

Creativity works differently in women and men, and women are most creative when they tap into the process that is unique to their own nature—a holistic, "spiraling" approach. The book is a self-help manual, both inspirational and practical, for igniting female creative fire. Ealy encourages women to acknowledge their own creativity, often in achievements they take for granted. She also gives a wealth of suggestions and exercises to enable women to recognize their own creative power and to access it consistently and effectively. Ealy holds a doctorate in behavioral science and consults with individuals and corporations on creativity.

NURTURING SPIRITUALITY IN CHILDREN
Author: Peggy D. Jenkins, $10.95 softcover

Children who develop a healthy balance of mind and spirit enter adulthood with higher self-esteem, better able to respond to life's challenges. This book offers scores of simple and thought-provoking lessons that parents can teach to their children in less than ten minutes at a time. Using items easily found around the house, each lesson provides a valuable message for children to take into their days and into their lives. The lessons are easy to prepare and understand, and each parent can alter the lessons to fit their own spiritual beliefs. The activities are adaptable for children from preschool to high school ages.

THE BOOK OF GODDESSES
Author/illustrator: Kris Waldherr
Introduction: Linda Schierse Leonard, Ph.D., $17.95 hardcover

This beautifully illustrated book introduces readers of all ages to twenty-six goddesses and heroines from cultures around the world. In the descriptions of these archetypal women, the author weaves a picture of the beauty, individuality, and unique strength which are the birthright of every girl and woman. Beautiful to look at and inspiring to read, this book is a stunning gift for goddess-lovers of all ages.

KNOW YOUR TRUTH, SPEAK YOUR TRUTH, LIVE YOUR TRUTH

Author: Eileen R. Hannegan, $12.95 softcover

To be truly yourself, you need to have an authentic integration of the mental, emotional, physical, and spiritual truths of self. This book offers a simplified formula of the ancient truths that escort an individual into personal and spiritual wholeness. The three-part program assists individuals in discovering the truth of who they truly are and thereby in living a more authentic life.

YOU CAN HAVE IT ALL

Author: Arnold M. Patent, $16.95 hardcover

Joy, peace, abundance—these gifts of the Universe are available to each of us whenever we choose to play the real game of life: the game of mutual support. *You Can Have It All* is a guidebook that shows us how to move beyond our beliefs in struggle and shortage, open our hearts, and enjoy a life of true ecstasy. Arnold Patent first self-published *You Can Have It All* in 1984, and it became a classic with over 200,000 copies in print. This revised and expanded edition reflects his greater understanding of the principles and offers practical suggestions as well as simple exercises for improving the quality of our lives.

LETTERS FROM THE LIGHT: AN AFTERLIFE JOURNAL FROM THE SELF-LIGHTED WORLD

Author: Elsa Barker; Editor: Kathy Hart, $12.95 hardcover

In the early part of this century, a woman begins a process of "automatic writing." It is as though someone takes over her hand and writes the document. Days later she finds out that the man has died thousands of miles away, and she is now serving as a conduit as he tells of life after death through her. His message: There is nothing to fear in death, and the life after this one is similar in many ways to the one we already know, even though we will be much more able to recognize our freedom. Readers of the book, originally published in 1914, invariably concur that the book removed from them the fear of dying.

To order or to request a catalog, contact:
BEYOND WORDS PUBLISHING, INC.
4443 NE Airport Road
Hillsboro, OR 97124-6074
503-693-8700 or 1-800-284-9673

Beyond Words Publishing, Inc.

Our corporate mission:

....

Inspire to Integrity

Our declared values:

....

We give to all of life as life has given us.

We honor all relationships.

Trust and stewardship are integral to fulfilling dreams.

Collaboration is essential to create miracles.

Creativity and aesthetics nourish the soul.

Unlimited thinking is fundamental.

Living your passion is vital.

Joy and humor open our hearts to growth.

It is important to remind ourselves of love.